W9-BSC-811

THE

NOW
HABIT

Also by Neil A. Fiore:

The Road Back to Health:
Coping with the Emotional Side of Cancer

With Susan C. Pescar:

Conquering Test Anxiety

THE
NOW
HABIT

A Strategic Program for

Overcoming Procrastination and

Enjoying Guilt-Free Play

NEIL A. FIORE, Ph.D.

Jeremy P. Tarcher/Putnam
a member of
Penguin Putnam Inc.
New York

Most Tarcher/Putnam books are available at special quantity
discounts for bulk purchases for sales promotions, premiums,
fund-raising, and educational needs. Special books or book excerpts
also can be created to fit specific needs.
For details, write Putnam
Special Markets, 375 Hudson Street
New York, NY 10014

Jeremy P. Tarcher/Putnam
a member of
Penguin Putnam Inc.
375 Hudson Street
New York, NY 10014
www.penguinputnam.com
Library of Congress Cataloging in Publication Data

Fiore, Neil A.
  The now habit.

  Bibliography.

  1. Procrastination.   2. Play—Psychological aspects.
I. Title.
BF637.P76F56   1989   158'.1   88-24864
ISBN 0-87477-504-3 (pbk.)

Designed by Brett Palmer

Manufactured in the United States of America
20 19 18 17 16 15 14 13 12

Cover design: Deborah Daly

This book is dedicated to all those people who had the courage and perseverance to seek help with the frustrating problem of procrastination. It has been written for all the people who, in their quest for help, brought with them a battered sense of self-worth, a desire to save some part of themselves, and a burning conviction that they had some good work to contribute. But most especially, this book is for Elizabeth.

Contents

Acknowledgments

This book came out of my own struggles with procrastination, motivation, and creativity; but in large part it is based on the experiences of thousands of clients and seminar participants who have shared their difficulties and their triumphs with me. I wish to acknowledge the contribution of these courageous individuals who repeatedly faced their fears and found within themselves the strength to try again. Their stories are told with the names, jobs, and situations changed to protect their privacy.

I also wish to acknowledge the constant support and love of my family and friends who offered me so many guilt-free meals and opportunities for guilt-free play. The staff at the University of California, Berkeley's Counseling Center deserves special mention for its support over many years. I want to thank Jeremy P. Tarcher, who believed in the early, rough draft of the manuscript and had the vision to see this book. I will continue to be grateful for the advice and help of my agents, Peter Beren and Jack Artenstein. Friends were invaluable in reading rough drafts and offering constructive criticism, but I especially appreciate the assistance of Jayne Walker and Harriet Whitman Lee. And I wish to acknowledge the editing skill and wise counsel of Hank Stine and the inspiration of Janice Gallagher, both of whom contributed greatly to the organization of this book.

Introduction

*Human nature has been sold short . . . [humans
have] a higher nature which . . . includes the
need for meaningful work, for responsibility,
for creativeness, for being fair and just, for
doing what is worthwhile and for preferring to
do it well.*

—ABRAHAM H. MASLOW
Eupsychian Management

Whether you are a professional, an entrepreneur, a middle
manager, a writer, or a student who wants to overcome
problems with procrastination—or if you simply want to
be more efficient in completing complex and challenging
projects—this program will help you get results. If you are
organized in your larger work projects, but find that the
small, essential tasks of everyday living get ignored, the
Now Habit will help you set priorities for, start, and complete these tasks as well. If you are a professional whose
busy schedule doesn't allow for leisure time, the Now
Habit strategic program will legitimize guilt-free play
while it improves the quality and efficiency of your work.

   If you suffer from extreme panic and blocks when
confronted by pressure to perform, this book will show
you how to overcome the initial terror so you can get
started. It will teach you to use empowering inner dia-

logue that leads to responsible choices, while avoiding ambivalant statements such as "should" and "have to."

The typical procrastinator completes most assignments on time, but the pressure of doing work at the last minute causes unnecessary anxiety and diminishes the quality of the end result. Procrastination is a problem that we all have in some areas of our lives, be it balancing the budget, filing a complicated legal brief, or painting the spare bedroom—anything we have delayed in favor of more pressing or pleasurable pursuits. We all have tasks and goals we attempt to delay—or totally escape.

FROM PROCRASTINATOR TO PRODUCER

The procrastination habit catches people in a vicious cycle: get overwhelmed, feel pressured, fear failure, try harder, work longer, feel resentful, lose motivation, procrastinate. The cycle starts with the pressure of being overwhelmed and ends with an attempt to escape through procrastination. As long as you're caught in the cycle, there is no escape. You can't even enjoy the recuperative and creative benefits of guilt-free leisure time. Suddenly, any time spent on play—and even time spent on more enjoyable work—feels like an uneasy shirking from what you *should* be doing. By negatively affecting the way you think and feel about work, leisure, yourself, and your chances for success, procrastination becomes a part of your identity.

Instead, you can cultivate the Now Habit: the ability to put aside the fear of failure, the terror of feeling overwhelmed, and low self-esteem, and focus your mind on what you can start *now.* The skills and strategies of the Now Habit program will let you think of yourself as a producer, feel like a producer, and act like a producer.

A NEW DEFINITION OF PROCRASTINATION

Dozens of books offer pop-psychology theories about why people procrastinate. They encourage self-criticism by giving you additional negative labels, and they imply that you're lazy by making greater demands for discipline and organization. But there's a big difference between just diagnosing what's wrong and providing a system that enables you to correct it. People who have been procrastinating for years on major life goals are already pretty good at self-criticism. What they need are positive, practical techniques for getting beyond the stumbling blocks and on to achieving their goals.

Some books offer prosaic advice such as "break it into small pieces" or "set priorities." You already know this. You've heard the advice, you have the knowledge—you may even have paid dearly for it. But this kind of advice isn't helpful because it misses the point: you would do these things if you could, if it were that simple.

People don't procrastinate just to be ornery or because they're irrational. They procrastinate because it makes sense, given how vulnerable they feel to criticism, failure, and their own perfectionism.

To overcome procrastination you need a positive attitude about the human spirit. This spirit's inherent motivation and driving curiosity has gotten us out of our caves and into condos, up from the comfort of crawling to the risks of standing and walking. The human spirit drives us to what Maslow calls our "need for meaningful work, for responsibility, and for creativeness." If we can harness it, it will ease the fears that cause procrastination and open entirely new horizons for human achievement.

The Now Habit is based on the fact that somewhere in your life there are leisure activities and forms of work that you choose to do without hesitation. You are more than "a procrastinator." You do not procrastinate twenty-four hours a day. When you turn your attention toward what you love to do—activities that foster your spontaneity, motivation, and curiosity—you know that you are more than a procrastinator, more than just lazy. With these experiences you can begin to shed your identity as a procrastinator and reconnect with your innate human drive to produce.

If early training has caused you to associate work with pain and humiliation, then just approaching an intimidating or unpleasant task can bring on a reliving of criticism, not only from your current boss but from parents, previous bosses, and teachers. Every insecurity bubbles up to your consciousness as you think about working on some project you feel you're no good at. Pain, resentment, hurt, and fear of failure have become associated with certain kinds of tasks. When life seems to hold too many of these tasks it's as if you're driving with the brakes on; you've lost your motivation and doubt your own inner drive to get things done. At this point your self-criticism seems justified. You're likely to think of yourself as a chronic procrastinator—someone doomed to experience anxiety and self-reproach when faced with certain kinds of projects.

Your first step toward breaking the procrastination habit and becoming a producer involves redefining procrastination and coming to a new understanding of how and why we use it. Procrastination is not the cause of our problems with accomplishing tasks; it is an attempt to resolve a variety of underlying issues, including low self-esteem, perfectionism, fear of failure and of success, indecisiveness, an imbalance between work and play, ineffective goal-setting, and negative concepts about work and self.

A complete treatment of procrastination must address the underlying blocked needs that cause a person to resort to procrastination. The Now Habit starts with a new definition:

> *Procrastination is a mechanism for coping with the anxiety associated with starting or completing any task or decision.*

From this definition it follows that those most vulnerable to procrastination are those who feel the most threatened by difficulty in starting a project; criticism; failure; and the loss of other opportunities that may result from committing to one project.

THE NOW HABIT

Advice such as "just do it," "try harder," and "get organized" is based on the old definition: "Your problem is procrastination. If only you weren't so lazy you could do it." Well-meaning parents, teachers, writers, and friends will worsen the problem by adding: "This is a really tough job. You're going to have to work really hard. No fooling around. No time for friends and vacations until this is completed." The message they communicate is: "Life is dull and hard. There's no time for fun. Work is dreadful, yet it must be done." This old model of work and life is similar to Woody Allen's "Life is hard, and then you die," or Scott Peck's "Life is difficult . . . you need to learn discipline."

This program is based on more positive definitions of life, work, human potential, and procrastination that are more in keeping with psychologist Abraham Maslow than with Sigmund Freud. It has greater faith in human nature, and therefore it goes beyond the typical "how to" book by putting you in touch with the deeper anxieties about failure, perfectionism, and the limits of your ability that lead you to procrastinate.

The Now Habit program emphasizes healing the underlying self-alienation—the working against yourself—that results from early training and cultural conditioning. It cuts through the crippling assumptions of the Puritan work ethic—that your production determines your worth—and the negative Freudian views of human drives—that a "lower self" must be subdued and disciplined by a higher, civilized self. Instead, the Now Habit reestablishes a working relationship within yourself that lessens inner conflict and allows you to engage your whole self in your task.

By giving you the tools to create inner safety and positive inner dialogue, it helps you to lessen the fear of being imperfect and enables you to take risks and start sooner.

Because practical application of this positive philosophy to work situations is so rare, you will find few direct references listed in this book. The underpinnings of this book are in somewhat less functional, but seminal, works such as Matthew Fox's *Original Blessing,* Jean Shinoda Bolen's *The Tao of Psychology: Synchronicity and the Self,* Susan Griffin's *Pornography and Silence: Culture's*

Revenge Against Nature, and Gerald Jampolsky's *Love Is Letting Go of Fear.*

The Now Habit is a *strategic* system—that is, it goes beyond tactical advice and presents a plan based on the dynamics of procrastination and motivation. The program shows you how to shift gears into a higher level of functioning so you can go faster, more efficiently. It shows you how scheduling more guilt-free play in your life can attack the underlying causes of procrastination by lowering resentment toward work, making it easier to start working, improving the quality of work, and stirring motivation. With this strategy you will be able to work virtually free of stress and enjoy your leisure time free of guilt. The Now Habit program will provide you with powerful tools for overcoming procrastination.

- **Creating safety** will show you how to put a psychological safety net under your high-wire act so that you can lessen your fear of failure and learn how to bounce back from mistakes with renewed purpose.

- **Reprogramming negative attitudes through positive self-talk** will help you to identify your negative messages to yourself and discover how they adversely affect you, while developing positive phrasing that directs your energy toward task-oriented thoughts and rapid solutions.

- **Using the symptom to trigger the cure** will show you how to use old habits to evoke and strengthen the formation of new, positive habits.

- **Guilt-free play** teaches you how to strategically schedule your leisure time in order to shift the pressure from work to play, and create a subconscious urge to return to work.

- **Three-dimensional thinking and the reverse calendar** will show you how to control the terror of being overwhelmed by important tasks by creating a step-by-step calendar of your path to achievement, with adequate time to rest and to fully appreciate your accomplishment.

- **Making worry work for you** will show you how to develop alternative plans for achieving your goals and strengthen confidence in your ability to face the worst that could happen.

- **The Unschedule** lets you see the freedom awaiting you through prescheduled guilt-free play, creates a realistic image of the amount of time available, and gives you a built-in time clock for recording quality time on projects to let you see how much you've accomplished.

- **Setting realistic goals** helps you to clear your mind of guilt-producing goals that cannot be worked on in the present, while directing your energies toward the few worthwhile goals that deserve your attention now.

- **Working in the flow state** gets you beyond stress and low motivation to a state of focused energy, interest, and concentration within two minutes or less—letting you know that regardless of how you feel about your project, within moments you will be working at your most productive and creative level.

- **Controlled setbacks** will prepare you for setbacks so that you quickly turn them into opportunities, anticipate the temptation to procrastinate, and build persistence into your overall plan for achievement.

EXPECT A MARVELOUS CHANGE

While many of the strategies described here are not new, what you will find to be new, even revolutionary, is that finally you have the means to apply these powerful strategies to the practical issues of your life. Armed with techniques for focusing on results and for recognizing and avoiding old pitfalls, you will discover yourself feeling positive and confident in situations that previously caused stress and procrastination. You will even discover that you are less critical and more supportive of yourself, capable of replacing old criticisms with positive, task-oriented directives and rechanneling the frustration of procrastination into successful production.

Since completing my doctorate in 1973, I have worked with hundreds of clients and dozens of organizations in creating a strategy that can lead participants to dramatically improved performance, freedom from destructive behavior, and enhanced self-esteem and confidence. I have also used this system to find the time in an already busy week to write articles for *The New England Journal of Medicine, Science Digest,* and *Reader's Digest,* and to write my previous book, *The Road Back to Health,* in twenty *quality* hours a week for a year and a half while maintaining a commitment to *guilt-free* time for friends and the training necessary to run three half-marathons. And this system has been used successfully by clients who considered themselves to be recalcitrant procrastinators.

We will not be guilty of Mark Twain's complaint:

"Everybody talks about the weather, but nobody does anything about it." While we can't do much about the weather, we can start today to do something about procrastination.

The Now Habit program for quality work and guilt-free play has worked for me and my clients. It can work for you too!

1

Why We Procrastinate

*The healthy individual has an appetite for
fruitful activity and for a high quality of life.*

—GEORGE BERNARD SHAW

Your strategic program begins with identifying your procrastination patterns so you can apply the appropriate techniques for replacing them with the effective work patterns of producers.

WARNING SIGNS OF PROCRASTINATION

These six warning signs will help you quickly determine if you have significant difficulties with procrastination, goal achievement, or inefficient work habits.

1. Does life feel like a long series of obligations that cannot be met? Do you
   - keep an impossibly long "to do" list?
   - talk to yourself in "have to's"?
   - feel powerless, with no sense of choice?
   - feel agitated, pressured, continually fearful of being caught procrastinating?

- suffer from insomnia and have difficulty unwinding at night, on weekends, and on vacations (if in fact you take vacations)?

2. Are you unrealistic about time? Do you

- talk about starting on projects in vague terms such as "sometime next week" or "in the fall"?
- lose track of how you spend your time?
- have an empty schedule without a clear sense of commitments, plans, subgoals, and deadlines?
- chronically arrive late at meetings and dinners?
- fail to take into account the actual time it takes to drive across town during rush hour?

3. Are you vague about your goals and values? Do you

- find it difficult to stay committed to any one person or project?
- have difficulty knowing what you really *want* for yourself, while clear about what you *should* want?
- get easily distracted from a goal by another plan that seems to be free of problems and obstacles?
- lack the ability to distinguish between what's the most important use of your time and what's not?

4. Are you unfulfilled, frustrated, depressed? Do you

- have life goals that you've never completed or even attempted?
- fear always being a procrastinator?
- find that you're never satisfied with what you accomplish?
- feel deprived—always working or feeling guilty about not working?
- continually wonder "Why did I do that?" or "What's wrong with me?"

5. Are you indecisive and afraid of making a mistake? Do you

- delay completing projects because you try to make them perfect?
- fear taking responsibility for decisions because you're afraid of being blamed if something goes wrong?
- demand perfection in your work?
- expect to be above mistakes and criticism?
- worry endlessly about "what if?"

6. Are low self-esteem and lack of assertiveness holding you back from becoming productive? Do you

- blame outside events for your failures because you're afraid to admit to any deficiencies?
- believe "I am what I do" or "I am my net worth"?
- feel ineffective in controlling your life?
- fear being judged and found wanting?

If you can relate to most of these categories the chances are you already know that you have real problems with procrastination. If you see only some of these warning signs in yourself you may be procrastinating in some areas of your life while remaining in control in most areas.

If you've ever been caught in a procrastination cycle you know the personal cost you pay in your life: missed deadlines for job and school applications, lost sales because of a failure to follow up on calls, and broken relationships due to continual lateness and cancelled plans. But even if you avoid these extremes and can responsibly meet obligations and deadlines, you may still suffer from problems with procrastination. The fact is that most of us who consider ourselves procrastinators meet deadlines and avoid serious penalties. But we feel so rushed, so pressured, and so unhappy with the results that we have to admit we have inordinate difficulties with any frightening or unpleasant task. Our real distress comes from the constant anxiety of delaying, from guilt about the inferior quality of projects completed at the last minute, and from deep regrets about life's missed opportunities.

A POSITIVE VIEW OF
THE HUMAN SPIRIT

"Why do you procrastinate?" The most frequent response to this question is "Because I'm lazy." Yet even the worst procrastinators have motivation and energy for some areas of their lives—sports, hobbies, reading, taking care of others, music, dancing, political debate, investments, gardening. So-called procrastinators and self-labeled procrastinators can be found in every walk of life, accomplishing much in those arenas where they have chosen to devote themselves, but totally unable to get started in others.

The Now Habit perspective does not accept that laziness, disorganization, or any other character defect is the reason you procrastinate. Nor does it accept the assumption that people in general are innately lazy and passive, and therefore need pressure to motivate them. The Now Habit is based on what Suzanne Kobasa of the University of Chicago calls "those psychological orientations that emphasize human initiative and resilience." Her research on "The Hardy Personality" tells us that the more optimistic interpretations of human functioning are often left out of theories about how people cope. Likewise, in *Anatomy of an Illness* and *The Healing Heart*, Norman Cousins informs us that modern medicine has virtually ignored the positive aspects of the body's resilient healing system, preferring to focus on disease. He says that humor and positive emotions and thoughts have healing potential, just as negative thinking contributes to the breakdown of our health. The Now Habit applies a similar positive attitude about the human spirit to the problem of procrastination.

"If human nature has this ability to be so positive and active, then why do we procrastinate?" you might ask. One explanation is offered by Denis Waitley, the author of *The Psychology of Winning* and *The Joy of Working*, who defines procrastination as "a neurotic form of self-defensive behavior" aimed at protecting one's self-worth. That is, we procrastinate when we fear a threat to our sense of worth and independence. We only act lazy when our natural drive for fruitful activity is threatened or suppressed. "No one does it to feel bad," says Waitley, "but to temporarily relieve deep inner fears."

What are the deep inner fears that cause us to seek such unproductive forms of relief? Dr. Theodore Rubin in his book *Compassion and Self-Hate* suggests that it is the fear of failure, the fear of being imperfect (perfectionism), and the fear of impossible expectations (being overwhelmed) that prevent us from acting on and attaining humanly possible goals and relationships. Having a fear of failure means you believe that even the smallest error could be evidence that you are a worthless and awful person. Having a fear of being imperfect means that it is difficult for you to accept yourself as you are—imperfect and human—and therefore you feel any criticism, rejection, or judgment by others as a threat to your very tenuous grasp on perfection. Having a fear of impossible expectations means fearing that even after you've worked hard and achieved the goals set for you, your only reward will be continually higher and more difficult goals to achieve, with no rest and no time to savor your achievements.

These fears, Dr. Rubin says, keep us from reaching a level of life where we feel compassion and respect ourselves *now*—for who and where we are now. This compassion for ourselves is essential in overcoming the underlying causes of procrastination. It means understanding that procrastination is *not* a character defect; rather, it is an attempt—albeit an unsatisfactory one—at coping with the often incapacitating fear of having our worth held up for judgment.

The fear of judgment is the key fear that stems from over-identifying who you are, your worth as a person, with your work. From this fear follows the counterproductive drive toward perfectionism, severe self-criticism, and the fear that you will deprive yourself of free time in order to satisfy some unseen judge.

OUR WORST CRITIC: OURSELVES

Perched nervously on the sofa in my waiting room was a young woman who looked very much like a lost child. She clutched her handbag tightly and sat scrunched forward on the edge of her seat as if in pain. When I called her name, Clare brightened and tried to smile, but it came across as anxious and awkward. As she stood I could see that Clare was a tall, well-dressed woman in her late twenties who could rapidly drop her childlike appearance and look her true age.

Once we reached my office, Clare resumed her childlike look. Hunched over, she said meekly, "I may be fired from my job. I've received a poor performance evaluation; they'll fire me if I don't improve. I feel awful. I've never failed at anything in my entire life."

This was Clare's first responsible position, a promising one with a rapidly expanding company involved in marketing medical products. For more than thirty minutes she poured out her problems with procrastination: a story of embarrassment, humiliation, and self-contempt, about constant anxiety, continual feelings of being out of control, missed deadlines, and rushed projects that left no time to check for obvious errors.

"I just couldn't face all the demands they made on me. There was so much they wanted me to learn," Clare told me. "There were continual interruptions and no clear guidelines. I didn't know what they wanted from me. I felt so stupid, so incompetent. After a while I just couldn't get started, even though I really wanted to. I was so afraid of making a mistake. Whenever I tried to begin one of my projects I'd hear my boss's voice telling me how to do it right and how important it was. My way of doing things is so different from his.

"When I first got the job everyone was eager for me to start. There was a huge backlog from Janet, the person who had my job before me. But I'd just begin to get into it—developing my own ideas—when someone would ask me how I was doing. When I would stupidly show them my work, they'd proceed to point out how tough it was going to be to fill Janet's shoes. After a while I stopped asking for help and stopped showing my work to anyone. When I'd get stuck on something, I'd get so nervous and depressed I'd just put it away, take a coffee break, or talk to someone about the weather—anything to try and get away from the nervousness.

"But it didn't start with this job. Procrastinating isn't new for me, I've had this problem since grade school. I knew that my difficulties with procrastination would always catch up with me. I have an ulcer that started in high school. Even then I would worry about turning in a project for fear that it would be awful and mediocre—just average."

As Clare spoke the words *mediocre, just average,* a look of disgust crossed her face. I decided this would be a good time to interrupt. She had spent quite a bit of time describing herself as the victim and the scared, helpless child, but at this moment she had become the judge and the critic. Not very positive roles, but ones with more energy and potential for movement than the part of her that felt so devastated by a poor performance evaluation.

" 'Just average' is pretty awful for you, isn't it, Clare?" I asked. "It makes you feel miserable, as if you're worthless. Sounds as if you can be pretty tough on yourself. You expect all your work to be superior, maybe even perfect, and when it isn't, you get disgusted with yourself. It's as if your projects become more than just work to be taken care of; for you they become reflections of your worth as a person. I would bet that when your work is judged 'average,' you tell yourself you're bad—as if *you're* being judged. Where did you learn to talk to yourself that way?"

My question puzzled Clare, and she took a moment to think. "It's been that way ever since I can remember. I've been raised to believe that you should be the best in everything you try; anything less is failure. If I failed I'd feel like a failure."

Then Clare told me about where she had learned to think of herself as part judge and part lazy child. "I'm the youngest of four. My two brothers and sister are fairly successful, and of course my father's *really* successful and wealthy, and my mother is well liked and very good at everything she does. I've always felt as if I had to play catch-up and that I never could—they were always so much better at everything. I think I would have liked to go into medicine, but that's so competitive anyway and my oldest brother had already chosen that. Ever since I can remember, they all made fun of me if I asked for help with my homework. I was always expected to do well and have no problems. I suppose they thought they were showing me how bright I was. There was never any praise for my accomplishments, even when I worked very hard. But there was plenty of criticism when I'd blow it and get a B in history or something. I always felt as if someone was looking over my shoulder, worried about how well I was doing or how smart I was.

"All my life I've been told I have to discipline myself to be really good at the piano, at ballet, at science. I felt I had to force myself to do these things for them even though I wanted to be outside playing with the other kids. It seemed so important to my parents that I be good at something special. I wanted them to be happy, so I really tried *for them*. I've done okay, but never really special. Never someone they could be proud of. No matter how hard I'd try, I'd get so nervous on tests and interviews that I could never do my best. I've always felt that if there wasn't so much pressure—just a little more time—I could do really well. But it always turns out average. I hate being average. But isn't it that way for everybody?"

This early family pattern is typical of many procrastinators. Praise is often withheld because "it might go to your head," leaving the child with a sense that their efforts are *never good enough*. There seems to be no way of pleasing their parents or teachers. Early in life they learn that all they can expect from finishing a project is criticism or so-called constructive feedback on how it might be improved. What's clearly being communicated is: "There's no rest for you. You'll always need to keep trying. Life and work are hard; it won't be easy for you; you have a lot more work to do before you can rest on your laurels; you'd better get used to things getting tough because adulthood is even worse than childhood; and while you're out having fun, some catastrophe is lurking around the corner, waiting to surprise you."

Her early training taught Clare that part of her was lazy and that this part would need discipline, pressure, and threats in order to do all the hard work that awaited her. She learned to take for granted that a judgmental and authoritarian part of her would have to push and threaten a lazy and childlike part. For Clare, being in constant conflict with herself was the only way she knew how to be. I wanted to challenge at least two of the counterproductive assumptions Clare's story revealed: the feeling that *she* had to force *herself*—that there needed to be an inner conflict; and that this constant conflict is normal, the way everybody lives—as if it's part of human nature to be lazy.

"I guess that's the way it is for many people, Clare," I said. "But believe me, it's not that way for everybody. And I don't believe that it was that way for you all of the time. I'd bet that at one time, when you were a little girl, everything you did was just fine, perfect in fact. Every sound you uttered was greeted with applause and a look of encouragement—a reassuring smile that you would do just fine. Everybody gave you time to learn in your way, at your own pace, in effect saying, 'We love you just the way you are.' "

Tears welled up in Clare's eyes and she wept, then apologized, "I'm sorry. I didn't mean to cry. I promised myself I wouldn't cry. I feel so stupid. I don't even know why I'm crying."

"Could it be that it's been a long time since you felt that unconditional acceptance?" I asked. "Maybe it's also been a long time since *you* were that approving of yourself. Notice how quickly you brought in that judging voice that says, 'It's stupid to cry. There's no logical reason to cry. Now stop that and apologize.' You've learned that voice very well, maybe too well. Where did you learn to talk to yourself in such a tough, critical way?"

I wanted to alert Clare to her negative "self-talk," which she could ultimately learn to control even when she couldn't control what others were saying to her. Feeling like the inadequate, incompetent victim had become so much a part of her identity that she simply assumed that the pressure of the critic was imposed from the outside. I was asking her to notice that *she* was the authoritarian judge. I explained to Clare that she probably learned that demanding voice as an attempt to ensure acceptance from parents who would withdraw their love and approval if she wasn't good. To do this she had to accept their belief that part of her could be bad, and that it would need constant watching and pressure to be made to work, even when it didn't want to. Thus Clare learned to talk to herself, not as a loving partner, but as a threatening and parental judge.

Clare's problems are prime examples of the consequences of what Alice Miller, in her book *For Your Own Good: Hidden Cruelty in Child-Rearing and the Roots of*

Violence, calls "poisonous pedagogy," which teaches the child low self-esteem and negative attitudes toward work. Clare had learned her attitudes about work and her abilities when she was too young to think for herself. Now that she was an adult, I wanted her to decide consciously which attitudes and assumptions made sense to her.

I also felt it was important for her to know the theories on which I based my approach to her problems. I told her that my work was based on a positive attitude about the human spirit, a belief that work and improvement are natural for the human body and mind, and that problems such as procrastination usually come about from suppression of that drive.

Once we had redefined some basic premises about work and procrastination in our first session, the next step was to discover the negative assumptions that underlay Clare's procrastination. I asked Clare to keep track of when and why she procrastinated for a few days to make her aware of when the old views were most likely to lead her into negative patterns. When she found herself procrastinating, she was to be alert to her habit of using procrastination to escape inner conflict and anxiety.

From the entries in her log, Clare made a list of her most frequent negative self-statements. From these we developed positive challenges to replace them and to redirect her focus toward the task at hand, rather than to questions of her ability or worth.

We still had a lot of work to do to rebuild Clare's confidence and to prepare her for negative feedback from her boss. But once she had a strategy that got rid of her worst critic, herself, we were able to lessen Clare's resistance to authority, fear of failure, perfectionism, and fear of success.

With the use of the Now Habit system, Clare got

beyond her image of herself as a procrastinator. She was able to focus on her accomplishments, her strengths, her innate drive for quality work, her intellectual curiosity, and her desire to improve whatever situation she was in. Having become her own source of approval, Clare grew less dependent on external judgments of her worth and was able to face work without procrastinating. She had unlearned her need to procrastinate and could now start thinking, feeling, and acting like a producer.

PROCRASTINATION IS REWARDING

In my work with thousands of procrastinators I have discovered that there is one main reason why we procrastinate: it gets rewards. In the case of Clare, who had many underlying reasons for seeking procrastination as a refuge, she learned to use procrastination because it effectively lessened her fear of being judged.

The main reason we learn any habit, as Drs. Frederick Kanfer and Jeanne Phillips tell us in *Learning Foundations of Behavior Therapy*, is that even a seemingly counterproductive habit like procrastination is immediately followed by some reward. Procrastination reduces tension by taking us away from something we view as painful or threatening. The more painful work is for us, the more we will try to seek relief through avoidance or through involvement in more pleasurable alternative activities. The more we feel that endless work deprives us of the pleasure of leisure time, the more difficult we will find it to start working.

In a sense we become addicted to using procrastination as a way to temporarily reduce the anxiety associated with certain tasks. If the work we thought we had to do later proves to be unnecessary, we have a justification and a double reward for procrastinating. Not only did we use procrastination to cope with our fears, we also discovered that it's a way to conserve energy. We learn that in some situations it makes sense to procrastinate, and we're even rewarded for it.

There are many ways in which normal delaying is rewarded and learned as a way of solving problems:

- Occasionally a postponed, boring task is completed by someone else.

- If you delay long enough making a decision about buying something, it will eventually reward you by either going on sale or going out of style.

- Procrastination often goes unpunished; in fact, somewhere in almost everyone's childhood is the experience of great anxiety about not preparing for an exam, only to have that enormous tension ecstatically relieved by the news that a storm or a strike has closed your school—thereby teaching you to procrastinate in hope of a similar miracle occurring again.

- When you took some time to cool down, you were able to avoid serious arguments with parents, teachers, bosses, and friends.

- Difficult decisions will eventually resolve themselves if you wait for additional information or allow the opportunities to pass.

Generally we are taught that procrastination is the problem, rather than a symptom of other problems. This diagnosis, instead of directing your efforts toward ending the cycle of pressure, fear, and procrastination, unfortunately makes matters worse by blaming you for choosing such an awful habit. Experts, bosses, and friends tell you that "you have to get organized. Just do it." And you try dozens of schedules and methods for scaring yourself into action, with marginal results, because the methods attack procrastination (and probably you as procrastinator) rather than the problems that led you to procrastinate in the first place.

When we identify our worth with our work ("I am what I do") we naturally are reluctant to face challenges and take risks without protection. If you believe that a judgment of your work is a judgment of yourself, then perfectionism, self-criticism, and procrastination are necessary forms of protection. Observing your hesitation to start or complete a project, supervisors and family members—often with good intentions—add encouragement, pressure, and threats to get you moving. As conflict builds between your internal fears of failure or imperfection and the external demands of others, you seek relief through procrastination. This can lead to a pernicious cycle:

Perfectionistic demands → fear of failure →
PROCRASTINATION → self-criticism → anxiety
and depression → loss of confidence → greater
fear of failure → stronger need to use PROCRASTI-
NATION

Procrastination does not start the pattern. From the perspective of the Now Habit, procrastination follows perfectionistic or overwhelming demands and a fear that even minor mistakes will lead to devastating rebuke and failure.

We can become addicted to the rewards of procrastination, learning to use it in three main ways: as an indirect way of resisting pressure from authorities; as a way of lessening fear of failure by providing an excuse for a disappointing, less-than-perfect performance; and as a defense against fear of success, by keeping us from doing our best. As we consider in more depth these major reasons for procrastinating, notice which ones reveal underlying causes of your own procrastination patterns.

Procrastination Can Express Resentment

You can use procrastination to get even with powerful authorities who place you in situations where your alternatives all seem negative. Pay the bills or go to jail, give up your vacation or lose your job. Procrastination in such situations reflects your resentment at the authority who placed you in this no-win dilemma. You feel like a victim whose life is controlled by others who make the rules. And you affirm your refusal to accept the rules by speaking about the unpleasant task in the victim's mantra—"I have to." "I have to pay the parking ticket. I have to have the presentation ready by Friday. But if I were in charge I wouldn't do it. If I were God there would be no parking tickets."

As a powerless victim you feel you can't openly rebel, because that would mean risking the probable consequences (anger and punishment), as well as losing the side benefits of the victim role (self-righteousness and martyrdom). But by procrastinating, you temporarily, secretly dethrone this authority. You can resist by dragging your feet and giving a halfhearted effort. If you are in a one-down position—a student, a subordinate, a private in the army—procrastination may be the safest way to exercise some power and control over your life. Bedridden patients, who appear totally helpless in comparison with the authority of the hospital staff, are seldom given opportunities to exercise control in their lives. Looking for some small way to express themselves in the controlled hospital environment, they procrastinate on taking their medication, complain about the food, and "refuse to *comply* with doctor's orders." Assembly-line workers and administrators at the bottom of the industrial hierarchy have been known to express their resistance to dictatorial managers by slowing down, by withholding initiative and following orders to the letter, and even by sabotaging the wheels of production.

Larry, a 55-year-old production supervisor in a tape manufacturing company, used procrastination to balance the inequities he saw between himself and his manager. He had been passed over for promotion several times. Over the years Larry had grown bitter about the younger people who were being promoted while he seemed destined to stay at the same level. Larry didn't realize how angry he was at Bill, the plant manager, but he did know that he couldn't *directly* express his feelings for fear of "blowing up, giving him a piece of my mind, and then losing my job." He felt stuck and temporarily solved the problem by procrastinating as an indirect expression of resentment and power. Without being totally aware of what he was doing, Larry began to ignore requests from Bill for reports and accounts. He would "forget," "misplace," and "feel ill" whenever he was asked to do anything for his boss.

Procrastination and laziness seemed to be the problems. But they were only surface attempts at coping with deep resentment and hurt. Larry felt powerless and stuck—too old to look for another job, he *had* to stick it out without ever saying anything about how he felt about the unfairness.

Self-empowerment and stopping the victim role would be the hardest parts of applying the Now Habit tools for Larry. Having made a conscious decision to stay with his job until retirement, Larry agreed that it made sense to challenge his victim message of "I have to" with the more empowering choices he could make each day. This was still his job, and he believed in his ability to do it well—in fact, better than any other employee. He recognized that his behavior had begun to confirm the negative opinion the manager had of him. Through a series of steps, Larry began to talk to himself in the language of "I choose," taking more responsibility for his job, breaking out of feeling like a victim who just follows the boss's orders. In an attempt to change the direction of his counterproductive struggle, Larry began to apply effective goal-setting, acknowledging where he was in the company rather than holding on to the fantasy of where he *should* be. It was difficult for Larry to admit that Bill was in charge and could affect his job; but denying this fact had kept him too long in a fatiguing and unpleasant struggle. The manager and Larry would never be friends again, but they didn't need to be enemies. Larry was determined to demonstrate this by reflecting an attitude of "I'm here to help you look good, not to be in your way." He even began to say hello to Bill for the first time in three years. To Larry's surprise, his boss recognized his initiative and change of attitude within one month of his decision to drop the victim role. The manager now considers Larry one of his most trusted employees, and Larry feels powerful in effecting a change in his work environment and his own feelings. His procrastination is no longer a problem because the underlying resentment and powerlessness have been removed.

Certainly others are frequently in positions of power to affect you and your job, and they might even try to judge your work or your skill. But they can never make you into a victim or a procrastinator. Only you can do that.

Procrastination Can Defend Against Fear of Failure

If you maintain extremely high standards for your performance and are critical of your mistakes, you will need to defend yourself from risky projects where the chances of failure are high. Perfectionism and self-criticism are, in fact, the chief causes of fear of failure. All of us at some time in our lives fail to achieve some of our goals, and that can be very disappointing and quite painful. But a failure to a perfectionist is like a small cut to a hemophiliac. It doesn't seem like much to a robust person, but it can be fatal to someone whose system is overly sensitive. And a perfectionist is even more sensitive to failure because having his or her work judged "average" is tantamount to being considered "a failure as a person." In extreme cases of perfectionism, there is no distinction between judgment of one's work and one's sense of value as a person.

The need to procrastinate as a protection against criticism and failure is particularly strong for those who feel they have to succeed at one specific goal, seeing no acceptable alternatives. Those who gain their sense of identity from many areas are more resilient when failing in any one area. For example, a professional tennis player is more likely to be upset by losing a match than is an amateur player for whom tennis is only one of many activities in the week. This has been borne out in studies by Yale psychologist Patricia W. Linville, who found that the more complex and varied your sense of self, the less likely you are to become depressed over stress in one area, because "you have these uncontaminated areas of your life that can act as buffers."

The person vulnerable to stress and procrastination is saying: "This project is me. My boss or client must love it, or I'll feel rejected as a person. If I can't make ten sales today I'm a failure. Whether I'm a winner or a loser in life will be determined by how well I do on this project." With your work bearing a weight as enormous as the determination of your worth and your future happiness, stress is inevitable. You need some form of escape to relieve the anxiety and to disengage your self-esteem from how well you do at this game of tennis, this exam, or this job. In such a predicament, procrastination can serve as a delaying action and as a way of getting you past your perfectionism. If you delay starting your work, you cannot do your best and so any criticism or failure will not be a judgment of the *real* you or your best effort. If you delay on making a decision, the decision will be made for you and you will not have to take responsibility if something goes wrong.

Performance anxiety and procrastination had made Elaine's life miserable. Whether it was a piano recital, an exam, a job interview, or a presentation at a meeting, Elaine died a thousand deaths. The mere thought of even a minor error caused her hours, often days, of panic and anxiety. Elaine was raised in a family of intense, high-energy, high achievers. Everywhere she looked on her family tree she saw alphabet soup: M.D.'s, Ph.D.'s, M.B.A.'s, J.D.'s, M.S.W.'s, and M.A.'s, all from "the best schools." She felt as if she worked in a fishbowl, a thousand eyes critically examining and judging her every move.

She had internalized their well-intended pressure to mean she had to be perfect, to never make a mistake. And this perfectionism was actually causing her to freeze at crucial moments and to ultimately avoid, through procrastination, any situation in which her performance might be evaluated.

When I first asked Elaine about her sense of innate worth, she was dumbfounded. "How can worth be innate?" she asked. "Where will it come from if it doesn't come from what I do?" When I asked her about those less capable than herself, she had to admit that they had worth and deserved respect in spite of their inability to perform as well as she, but it was difficult for her to apply a similar level of generosity to herself. But to avoid procrastination, she would need to create a contract with herself that whenever she made a mistake, she would remind herself of her worth, quickly forgive herself for not being perfect, and rapidly start over.

Procrastination Can Keep You from Facing Your Fear of Success

Fear of success involves three central issues: (1) you find yourself in conflict over the awful choice between advancement and friends; (2) success in completing a project means facing some painful disincentives to success, such as moving, looking for a new job, or paying back student loans; and (3) success means advancement to increasing demands and a fear of ultimate failure sometime in the future.

Conflict. When success in our career causes conflict in our relationships, procrastination can serve as an attempt to maintain contact with two worlds that seem diametrically opposed. Being unwilling to fully choose one over the other, we attempt to walk a middle ground by spending time with friends—sometimes resentfully—while procrastinating on work and suppressing the drive for success. In one of its more insidious forms, fear of success can express itself through unconscious self-defeating behavior.

The drive for success involves setting a goal, making it a high priority, and then investing time and energy toward its achievement. As the demands on your time and attention become greater, friends and family may come to resent your ambitions and your success. They may see your high-priority projects as indications that you care less for them and that their relationship with you is threatened. It often seems as if they are saying, "Choose between me or your career." As a client of mine put it, "I learned that you'll have more friends if you don't give them a reason to be jealous." If you find yourself in conflict between the support of friends and family or personal success, you have a terrible dilemma.

Working through tests quickly and easily in grammar school did not endear Dorothy to her schoolmates. They preferred to commiserate about how difficult a test was rather than to celebrate Dorothy's repeated successes. Nor did they appreciate that she was frequently the teacher's pet. Ambivalence and procrastination in doing her homework were the first signs that Dorothy was beginning to hold back for the sake of being popular. While Dorothy could never openly sabotage her performance, she did procrastinate in an attempt to avoid the hurt of being ostracized for her success.

By the time she reached adulthood, Dorothy had learned that success had its disadvantages. While it can't always be avoided, it should be approached warily. From her earliest experiences she had learned to fear competition, not because she could lose, but because she could win so easily. Being bright *and* athletic, oddly enough, made it very difficult for Dorothy to maintain friendships in grammar school and high school.

College was different for her, however. Here she was

more readily accepted. There were students who could compete at her level and some who even challenged her to test her limits. College offered her a greater opportunity to receive approval for her achievements. However, Dorothy found herself in the same class as her new boyfriend. This made her very anxious. She was still leery of endangering her new friendship with Peter. When Dorothy discovered that her grade for the class's first assignment was to be an A+, she quickly asked her professor to lower her grade so that she would not surpass, and presumably threaten, her boyfriend who had received only an A. Luckily, Dorothy had a professor and a boyfriend who were willing to support her success. She had to learn to trust in the true friendship of those interested in her advancement, even if others would turn away out of jealousy. Dorothy had to learn to make the difficult choice between wholehearted effort, with its probability of success, or the popularity offered by those who required her to be less successful. She learned that procrastination had become a convenient way of remaining ambivalent about this decision. Once Dorothy began facing the possible (and the imagined) consequences of success, she was able to make rapid decisions about her work and no longer needed procrastination.

Disincentives. Perhaps a more common fear of success results when we know that completing a particular project will be a mixed blessing, leading to both gains and losses. In business and in school, stagnation can develop when one completes a phase of career or education. There is a reluctance to leave what is familiar for the unknown, a reluctance to leave one level that has been mastered for a promotion into a new area where one must begin again the awkward and risky steps of the novice.

It had been difficult for John to leave the comfort of

the college campus for the "cold, cruel world." Upon graduating he quickly found a new home in a firm that treated him like one of the family. Within two years, however, John had learned everything he could in this small accounting firm. The job had become routine for him, and executive headhunters were making him tempting offers from large, competitive companies with challenging jobs. John was terrified of leaving another comfortable home for a job where he might feel like a small fish in a big pond. He coped with his fear of success by obsessive list-making of pros and cons that kept him procrastinating on a decision for two more years.

I found John's language—and thus, his thoughts—bound up with "should's" about advancing in the world and "I don't want to have to's" about leaving a secure job. John needed to start with a real choice and with full responsibility for his decision. But he was terribly afraid of making a mistake: "What if I find myself in over my head?" he repeatedly asked himself. "What if I want to go back to my old friends?"

John needed to confront his worst fears in such a way that he knew he would have options for his future and would not have to rely on everything (his job, his friendships) going perfectly. He also needed to know that if he failed, or even just had some difficulty with his new job, he would not criticize himself harshly for making a mistake. His demand on himself for perfection left little room for taking reasonable risks and bouncing back from unexpected difficulties. John also needed to learn that he could create his own "safety net," with which he could take small steps in exploring the possibility of success in a more challenging job.

Delayed Fear of Failure.   If you have been doing well, it is very likely that higher and higher expectations will be set for you. If you haven't had time for guilt-free play you may feel, "I really can't enjoy my success because still more is required of me. It takes the fun out of winning." I call this pattern the pole-vaulter syndrome. The chain of reasoning goes like this: You work hard and long for a very difficult goal, such as pole-vaulting sixteen feet. You're terribly afraid of failing, but the pressure of the crowd and your own expectations push you to try harder. You barely make the jump, but somehow you succeed. The applause of the crowd lasts for a few seconds and, while you're dusting yourself off, they're raising the bar to sixteen feet, six inches. With each successful jump it becomes more and more difficult to face the bar knowing the rewards are fleeting, the expectations for better performances are ever mounting, and the chances of failure are increasing. Dr. Derald Sue of Hayward State University in California calls this type of fear of success "delayed fear of failure."

> Fear of success can be seen as a fear of delayed failure: if you succeed in one task you're sure to be moved right on to a new competitive arena where failure is even more likely. The higher you go the more competitive it becomes—the greater the likelihood that you could fail. And if you can't stand failing, and you've tried your hardest already, that prospect is pretty frightening since there's no reserve left. With procrastination, though, you've covered yourself both ways: there's always an excuse, in case you don't perform as well as you'd hoped; and there's also some reserve left, if you still do succeed. . . . Success raises the anxiety that still more is going to be expected in the future . . . but procrastination gives some protection against that threat.

This pattern is often seen in movie and sports celebrities who burn out or who turn to drugs in an attempt to sustain superstar productivity. Resistance to the demands of success is often mixed with delayed fear of failure. Having achieved success, you would like to rest, but the crowd, the family, and the cost of your elevated lifestyle continually demand that you keep working hard.

Part of the delayed fear of failure, then, is that you will reach a point where you can no longer make yourself do what you've been telling yourself you *have to* do to maintain success. Your motivation has dried up. You can't seem to push yourself anymore.

At this point, you need more efficient ways of working, and you need the cooperation of your entire self. You'll need to drop the model of self-alienation that you learned as a child—the one that tells you part of you is lazy and needs to be forced to do things. You've been working against yourself, and resentment and fear of failure are draining you of the energy needed to achieve your goals effectively.

To unlearn this pattern you'll need to reduce the amount of pain and threat associated with your work, increase the rewards of work, use work to increase the pleasure of your playtime, and put yourself in control of reducing tension.

Procrastination has been learned, and it can be unlearned. Until now it's been a rewarding and necessary tool for escaping tasks that seem painful and depriving. Therefore, to gain control over procrastination, you need to develop alternative tools for coping with your fears, to make work less painful and less depriving. The Now Habit will give you the tools to overcome procrastination by making work more enjoyable—if not in itself, then by allowing greater enjoyment of leisure than you can get by procrastinating.

2

How We Procrastinate

*We all need an occasional whack on the side of
the head to shake us out of routine patterns, to
force us to rethink our problems, and to stimulate
us to ask new questions that may lead to other
right answers.*

—ROGER VON OECH
A Whack on the Side of the Head

Knowing *how* we procrastinate is even more important
than knowing *why*. We can use our awareness of negative
patterns that start a chain of counterproductive reactions
to redirect our energy toward forming positive habits.
Identifying how we go about doing anything is essential
to modifying or gaining control over it. Once we've identified specific negative behaviors, we can actually use
their onset to rechannel our behavior in a more desirable
direction.

KNOWING HOW YOU
SPEND YOUR TIME

The first step is easier than anything a book on procrastination has ever asked of you before: simply procrastinate
at your normal level for another week. I will teach you to
become aware of how and when you procrastinate. Just

observe yourself objectively, like an anthropologist who records the behavior and rituals of a foreign culture without making judgments. Don't judge yourself or analyze your behavior. For now, just concentrate on becoming aware of your current behavior patterns.

Observe where your time is going. What are you doing when you're really productive? And note how that differs from when you're busy all the time but producing nothing. Difficulties in gauging how much time it takes to complete a project, to travel across town, to make it to a meeting on time, are often part of procrastination. Realistic time management and a structure for focusing on commitments are necessary tools for making the transformation from procrastination to production. If you find yourself chronically late, overwhelmed with details, surprised by deadlines, procrastinating on dozens of projects, and with insufficient time for recreation and relationships, you have a time-management problem.

There are many theories about why humans have difficulty managing their time. But the difficulties remain a fact for most of us, regardless of the reason. We need a structure to keep us aware of the passage of time and how we spend it.

Keeping an inventory of every waking activity is a way to gain control over where your time goes. Davis, Eschelman, and McKay recommend in *The Relaxation and Stress Reduction Workbook* that you keep a record for three days, noting the total time spent on each activity. Then, through dividing that total by three, you arrive at an estimate of the average daily amount of time spent on each activity. Lawyers, architects, consultants, and other professionals use a similar procedure in determining the number of "billable hours" worked and for assigning them to the appropriate client.

To record the amount of time spent on your activities at work, at home, and with friends, you can create a schedule following Fran's schedule, outlined on pages 30 and 31. Divide your day into three or four segments to better assess when you are the most and the least productive. Record the time spent on each activity throughout your day.

Fran, an assistant manager in a clothing firm, came to me to gain control over time lost procrastinating on her job and to find more quality time with her husband and friends. Fran constantly felt rushed, with no time to concentrate on her major responsibilities, no real sense of achievement about what she had accomplished, and only halfhearted enjoyment of her free time. We discussed Fran's goals and established her priorities. Then Fran agreed to keep a record of how she spent her time. From this we could note any discrepancies between how much time she wanted to spend on her top priorities and how she actually spends her time.

Notice that in Fran's example, "work" is categorized A, B, or C, so that she takes credit for quality work only on high-priority projects. Fran does not count activities such as reading the mail or calling clients in her total time because she wants to reduce the time spent away from her major goals. By setting priorities in your work, you gain a clearer view of those tasks that really matter to you and your long-term goals. Alan Lakein, in *How to Get Control of Your Time and Your Life,* suggests using categories of most important (A), important (B), and least important (C). Certain "B" or "C" jobs, such as urgent tasks or committee work, can be used as a break from the more intense, and usually more valuable "A priority" activities. This system of categories and priorities lets you know when you're making progress on what's really important

Fran's Schedule

Activities	Time (in minutes)

I. Morning, at home (7:00 A.M.–9:15 A.M.)

listening to radio before getting out of bed	15
stretching, sit-ups, yoga	10
shower	15
dress	20
breakfast while watching TV	30
dropping off laundry, picking up laundry for evening, arranging papers for club meeting	15
commuting	30
Segment total	**2 hr., 15 min.**

II. Morning, at work (9:15 A.M.–12:45 P.M.)

chatting with boss	10
reading mail, newspaper	20
phone, outgoing calls	15
daydreaming, plans for shopping	10
clearing desk, looking for folders	15
break, coffee, socializing	15
WORK, LOW PRIORITY—C's	45
phone, incoming call	20
WORK, HIGH PRIORITY—A's	60
Segment total	**3 hr., 30 min.**

III. Afternoon, at work (12:45 P.M.–6:15 P.M.)

lunch, socializing	75
return phone calls	30
meeting	60
WORK, LOW PRIORITY BUT URGENT—C+'s	30
break	15
WORK, HIGH PRIORITY—A's	45

consultation	30
WORK, INTERMEDIATE PRIORITY—B's	30
cleaning up, organizing for tomorrow's meeting	15
Segment total	**5 hr., 30 min.**

IV. Evening, at home (6:15 A.M.–11:30 P.M.)

commute	30
shopping	20
socializing, reading mail	15
exercise	25
shower	10
preparing for/helping with dinner	30
dinner	45
TV	60
phone	20
paying bills, balancing checkbook	20
reading	30
cleaning up for sleep	10
Segment total	**5 hr., 15 min.**

TOTAL: 16 hr., 30 min.
work: 2 hr., 15 min.; exercise: 35 min.

and when you're just making activity—putting out fires—
without making much progress. Edwin Bliss, in *Getting
Things Done*, categorizes activities by noting their urgency and reminds us that what's urgent is not always the
best use of our time. Having too many urgent tasks indicates poor time management and avoidance of the really
important activities that pay off in the long term.

Fran and I reviewed how she spent her time on a
typical day and noticed several areas for improvement.
She decided that she wanted to get out of bed immedi-

ately and spend less time on breakfast. By eliminating television in the morning and evening on those days when she was pressed for time, Fran estimated that she could save 75 minutes a day and get to bed earlier. By taking care of personal errands in the evening instead of in the morning Fran could be better prepared and on time for work.

By tackling the "A priority" activities (budget, customer, and dealer issues that would have long-term effects on the company) first thing in the morning, she found that she could cut down on time wasted on the mail, telephone, and in casual conversations. In addition, Fran reviewed her goals to spend more leisure time with her friends and to have more time for reading and recreation. She found that if she changed her lunch routine two or three times a week to include a walk or a yoga or aerobics class (leaving enough time for a light meal), she was often more refreshed and productive in the afternoon than if she had eaten a large meal. This also helped free up some of the time in the evenings previously spent exercising.

Maintaining your own record for a few days will give you a pretty good estimate of how you spend your time. As you review a typical week's activities you can total the amount of time spent on the phone, reading the mail, eating, socializing, working, and so forth. This will reveal patterns that you may wish to change and others that you wish to encourage or start earlier in your day.

You may be alarmed to find that much of what transpires in your life is not directly related to high-priority tasks. Don't expect to find eight hours of quality work a day. Much of the legitimate activity in life is not directly related to productivity. For example, work in a large organization does involve socializing, meetings, and commu-

nication to maintain a team appro
mand. Simply look for areas of impro,
control over interruptions and lost time. W
ing machine (or secretary), telephone calls c.
turned at your convenience rather than handled as
come in, breaking your concentration and momentum.

Or you may find that, like many people, you take more than an hour to "settle in" before getting started. What would happen to your efficiency if you started on a high-priority project first thing in the morning, rather than reading the mail or making phone calls? To make changes, you'll need to break out of automatic pilot and start making conscious choices when you first enter your office in the morning. Use your record to identify the events that precede procrastination or low-priority work. Knowing which events trigger negative habits will help you switch to more productive activities.

Now that you've examined how you spend your time, you have a much clearer idea of the weak spots in your day that encourage procrastination. You may also discover that recording the amount of time spent on priority projects gives you greater control over where your time goes, makes it easier for you to enjoy leisure time free of guilt, and encourages you to do quality, concentrated work whenever you can.

THE PROCRASTINATION LOG

Keeping a record of how your time is spent will alert you to many areas of inefficiency and lost time, but it will not provide you with the cues in the actual work situation that signal the need for a change in focus if you are to avoid falling back into your old patterns. For that you'll need to

Procrastination Log

Date & Time	Activity & Priority	Thoughts & Feelings
2/6 9:30 A.M.	Income tax, A	I don't want to have to.
2/7 10:00 A.M.	Screen door, B	Can't I rest on Saturday?
2/9 3:15 P.M.	Speech, AAA	It has to be exceptional.
2/10 9:30 A.M.	Jones brief, A	I can't face Judge Smith.

keep a procrastination log, which links the avoided activity to a specific thought, justification, attempted solution, and resultant thought.

With some record of your *current* behavior and thoughts, you'll know where to take corrective action. Without a record it's almost impossible to learn from past mistakes. Think back to last week. Do you know what you did, how much time was lost, and what you were feeling that lead you to procrastinate? Probably not. That's why I strongly encourage you to make some record of your activities and thoughts or use the procrastination log. It provides a system to make it easier for you to gain control of your time and your behavior patterns.

Another of my clients, Frank, an insurance salesman, was very productive with the important projects of his life—he performed his job well, he met his appointments and deadlines on time, and he was available for his wife

Justification	Attempted Solution	Resultant Thoughts & Feelings
It's too nice out	Got one file, took a walk	Glad I got started and enjoyed my walk
Overburdened	Watched TV	Guilty; blamed self for laziness; fear wife's anger
I'm too anxious	Got coffee	Felt more anxious; felt bad about myself
Fear of mistakes	Worked on deposition instead	Cowardly; more pressure as time passes

and children. But his hatred of details and correspondence was catching up with him and making him feel like a procrastinator. His desk at home was perennially covered with overdue bills, uncashed checks, and unanswered letters, which frequently would be lost in the pile. Somewhere, under the pile of unfiled clippings, were photos that he had promised to send to his family in New York, and in one of the drawers there were rolls of film from last summer's vacation still waiting to be developed.

Why was a productive man like Frank procrastinating on sending photos to his mother? We examined Frank's procrastination log for evidence of the behaviors and thoughts that diverted him from tackling detail tasks. Frank discovered that whenever he saw that desk he felt overwhelmed with the work it represented and his mind quickly turned toward high-priority projects—exercise, building a table for his children, reading material from the office. In addition, the desk had become a painful reminder of all the people to whom he owed letters, of his own self-criticism about this one corner of disorganization in his otherwise orderly life. For Frank, small tasks had become lost in a formidable pile that was too easily avoided in favor of tasks that were more rewarding and had more easily identifiable steps.

By identifying the source of his problem, we were able to help Frank break the big job of "getting organized" into less threatening, bite-sized pieces. With the Now Habit tools, Frank was able to replace self-criticism for the messiness of the entire desk with a commitment to start now on accomplishing one task (such as finding the photos, placing them in an addressed, stamped envelope, and writing a letter) for a short period of time (such as fifteen to thirty minutes), and reorder his breaks and rewards so that they followed a short period of work rearranging the photos, gathering the bills together, or writing one letter.

That first week Frank sent off the photos to his mother, paid several lost bills, and set up vertical files for the items on his desk so he could see them quickly rather than having to shuffle through several piles. To maintain his momentum, Frank chose three times a week when he would spend at least one-half hour organizing and filing incoming mail, bills, and letters. This may sound too easy. The fact is that it is easy—after you've used the procrastination log to identify the attitudes and self-talk that are keeping you from getting started and then replaced them with a focus on one small step.

Even an elementary use of the log will give you important information about your procrastination patterns and self-statements. You will want to include as basic information the day and time that you procrastinated, the activity you postponed and its priority, your thoughts and feelings about the task, your reason for procrastinating, the type of procrastination you used, your attempts at reducing anxiety, and your resultant thoughts and feelings.

After a few days of recording your procrastination patterns, you'll be able to identify which thoughts lead toward achievement and which ones lead toward further delay and self-rebuke. Notice in the example how, in the first event, this person got one file for his income tax report and then took a walk, with the result that he felt good about starting and enjoyed his walk. In the second event, fixing the screen door, we can see how resentment about having free time interrupted by a chore led to feeling overburdened and resulted in procrastination, guilt, self-blame, and fear of a spouse's anger.

By breaking down your procrastination patterns in this way you equip yourself to target the thoughts and feelings that need to be guided toward production. You'll realize that the absurd lengths taken to procrastinate indicate how much pain you've trained yourself to associate with the task. You *know* how monumental the deprivation, self-criticism, and perfectionism have become if you find yourself compelled to clean the grout in your shower or organize your closets. When high-priority projects get replaced by low-priority items on your to-do list, you can take some solace in knowing that at least you're completing a chore. But you are meeting your need for control, organization, and accomplishment in distracting areas that offer only partial satisfaction. You will continue to procrastinate until you adopt a strategy that allows you to find full satisfaction in your high-priority projects.

Your procrastination log can also alert you to the *types* of situations in which you are most likely to procrastinate:

- detail activities (example #1): income tax, balancing the checkbook, arranging files, sorting customer records

- home chores (example #2): fixing the screen door, cleaning out the basement, clearing the desk, painting the bedroom

- performance tasks (example #3): giving a speech, presenting your product, confronting an employee

- big or dense projects (example #4): preparing a legal brief, an advertising campaign, or a training manual

By alerting yourself to the specific types of tasks that give you the most trouble, you will be better prepared to anticipate them and take action that will help you make progress on the task at hand.

Under the "thoughts and feelings" category of your procrastination log, note any underlying negative attitudes and beliefs that lead to feelings of victimhood, deprivation, pressure to be perfect, or fear of failure. These feelings, and the attitudes that cause them, get in the way of efficiently completing bothersome tasks. Note how they worked in the example:

- others are making you do something against your will (the income tax forms in #1 and the screen door in #2)

- pressure from yourself to give a perfect performance (the speech in #3)

- fear of mistakes and criticism (the image of appearing before the judge in #4)

Continue to record your procrastination behavior for two to three days and notice your typical patterns. Identify the fears and pressures you typically associate with certain types of projects. For example, notice how you might be mentally complicating a task so that it appears overwhelming. Be especially aware of how you talk to yourself and how your language leads to procrastination or production (the next chapter will address in depth the issue of our self-statements and how to change how we talk to ourselves).

Your procrastination log will alert you to your inner dialogue and how it is helping or hindering your goal achievement. Awareness of your inner dialogue and how it connects to your procrastination patterns will allow you to get the most out of the Now Habit strategy. The first major step out of procrastination is to become aware of how fear leads to your old patterns and how creating safety leads to productivity.

CREATING SAFETY: THE FIRST MAJOR STEP OUT OF PROCRASTINATION

To better understand how you learned to procrastinate, I invite you to use your imagination and to accept for a few minutes a metaphor in which the test or task in your life is to walk a board.

Situation A. The task before you is to walk a solid board that is thirty feet long, four inches thick, and one foot wide. You have all the physical, mental, and emotional abilities necessary to perform this task. You can carefully place one foot in front of the other, or you can dance, skip, or leap across the board. You can do it. No problem.

Take a minute to close your eyes, relax, and imagine yourself in that situation. Notice how you feel about this task. Are you scared or blocked in any way? Do you feel any need to procrastinate? Fear of failing or making a mistake cannot be an issue here, but you might find that you delay starting out of a need to assert your independence and to resist being asked to do even a simple task such as walking a board.

> **Situation B.** Now imagine that the task is just the same, to walk a board thirty feet long and one foot wide, and you have the same abilities; only now the board is suspended between two buildings 100 feet above the pavement. Look across to the other end of the board and contemplate beginning your assignment.

What do you feel? What are you thinking about? What are you saying to yourself? Take a moment to notice the differences in your reactions from situation A. Notice how rapidly your feelings about the task change when the height of the board changes and the consequences of falling are greater.

If your reactions are like those of most of my workshop participants, you may find yourself responding, "I'm thinking about the height. What if I fall? The consequences of falling or making a mistake would probably be death."

Of course, while you are focusing only on the danger of falling you are losing sight of the simplicity of the task and forgetting that just a moment ago you had all the ability to do it with no problems. The danger of a mistake is now so great that you must stop to consider this threat to your life. It's no longer just a job, a test, a project; it's your life, your future that's at stake. There's no way you can be calm now; you're already feeling the adrenaline rush of the stress response as you look over the edge, presenting to your mind and body the image of falling 100 feet. There's real reason to fear: "If I made a mistake I would die." Regardless of how simple the task, and regardless of how capable you are, that fear—that a mistake could mean the end of your life—makes it impossible to take that first step.

Ironically, on a psychological level you are often the one who raises the board off the ground by changing a straightforward task into a test of your worth, proof that you are acceptable, a prediction that you will be successful and happy or a failure and miserable. In most cases you are the one who confuses just *doing the job* with *testing your worth,* where one possible mistake would feel like the end of the world. When your early training leads you to believe that your self-worth is determined by your performance, you focus on psychological self-protection from fear of failing (and falling), rather than on just doing the job.

> **Situation C.** In this scene you are still on the board suspended between two buildings, 100 feet above the ground. The task remains simple and you still have all the ability necessary to do it, yet you remain frozen on your end of the board. While thinking about what to do, you suddenly notice that

the building supporting your end of the board is on fire.

What thoughts and feelings occur? How have you changed your focus from the previous situation? Remember, just a moment ago you were frozen in fright about the possibility of falling 100 feet. Do you find yourself thinking, "I've got to get across now. No time to worry about falling or doing it perfectly, I'll do it any old way I can. Dignity and embarrassment are no longer relevant."

Most people start thinking creatively about getting across that board by whatever imperfect means they can. Making a mistake and doing the job perfectly are quickly forgotten and workshop participants often say, "I'd scoot across that board on my bottom—on my hands and knees if I had to." It is only the dread of something worse that gets us beyond our dread of being less than perfect, of being judged, of facing who we really are and what we really can do.

Notice how quickly your feelings changed when you knew there was a more immediate and real danger than the possibility of falling. How did you do that? Are you surprised to find yourself creatively solving the problem of crossing the board, with little consideration of your fear of falling? A moment ago, the mere image of a life-threatening situation may have caused you stress. But notice how quickly your mind and body redirect your energy away from worry, ambivalence, and procrastination toward productive action once you've made a decision. (If the image of the fire was not a great motivator for you, see how your worries about the task and the dangers of falling change when you imagine that a small child is on the other side crying for your help.)

Now that you have an immediate time pressure, a real

deadline, you jump into the task with both feet, doing it any old way you can. You're no longer just facing a *possibility* or fear of pain and death, now you're confronting real pain and *certain* death. Now you find yourself unstuck and motivated. And that's how we use procrastination to get ourselves unstuck from a situation we created in the first place!

When you procrastinate, it's as if you are the one raising the board off the ground, getting yourself frozen, and then lighting that fire to create the pressure of a real deadline.

First you give a task or a goal the ability to determine your worth and happiness. "Getting this job, passing this test, dating this person will change my life and make me happy." When performance or the achievement of a specific goal becomes the sole measure of your self-worth, too much is at stake to just start working without some leverage, such as procrastination, to break the equation of self-worth = performance.

Psychologist Rich Beery of the University of California at Berkeley states that fear of failure stems from assuming that what we produce reflects our ability, and our ability in turn determines our worth as people. Procrastination allows us to break this terrible equation and resist being judged by our production because we never make a complete effort that reflects our full ability.

Through perfectionism you raise the task 100 feet above the ground, whereby any mistakes would be tantamount to death, so that any failure or rejection would be intolerable. You demand that you do it perfectly—without anxiety, with complete acceptance from your audience, with no criticism. Jane Burka and Lenora Yuen, in *Procrastina-*

tion: Why You Do It, What to Do About It, give the example of David, a lawyer for whom

> writing a legal brief for a case is the performance that measures not only his ability to be a good lawyer but also his value as a human being. If he works hard to prepare the brief and it isn't brilliant, he will be devastated—it means he is a *terrible* person who can't do *anything.* "I don't think I could stand it if I went all out and the brief still wasn't good enough."

You find yourself frozen with anxiety as your natural stress response produces adrenaline to deal with threats to your survival. The more issues you pile upon this task the more serious the threat if an error occurs. So in a series of "what if's" you create a catastrophic image of a row of falling dominoes—one mistake leading to the loss of a client, leading to the loss of a job, leading to failed attempts at ever finding another job, leading to the breakup of your marriage, and so on. With such images it doesn't take much to feel tension and stress and then to seek release through procrastination.

You then use procrastination to escape your dilemma, which brings the deadline closer, creating time pressure, a higher level of anxiety, and a more immediate and frightening threat than even your fear of failure or of criticism for imperfect work. You might even feel more powerful at this point; after all, you balanced out your anxieties and made them work for you. You also escape the terrible equation of self-worth = performance by delaying enough so that you cannot be tested on your real ability—that is, what you could do if you had enough time.

You also can use the scare tactic to create a sense of a real "have to," relieving you of responsibility for the decision and any possible mistakes. The fire or time pressure serves as a decision-maker as well as a motivator. A very convoluted and costly device, to be sure, but nevertheless it works to override the paralysis of your perfectionism and fear of failure. Once again you learn that procrastination makes sense and is rewarded. And it will keep you in this insidious cycle until you unlearn it and replace it with more effective and efficient methods of approaching work and worth.

> **Situation D.** You're back on the board again, 100 feet above the ground. There's no fire this time, but there is a net—a strong, supportive net, just beneath the board.

What are your feelings now? Can you imagine yourself walking that board, contemplating the completion of this task? "No problem," most people say. "I can do it now. It might even be fun. Even if I fell, I could bounce in the net."

You now know that if you fall the worst that could happen is that you might feel a little embarrassed. Falling no longer means death. A mistake does not mean the end of the world. You can recover from any fall. No single mistake would mean the end for you. You can always give yourself another shot at the task.

If you maintain perfectionist standards, then failing to achieve your goals or making a mistake can feel as if you're going to die. But maybe your job, your relationship, or your home is so important to you that losing it would feel like the end of the world. If so, you'll want to know how to create alternatives that allow you to bounce back from your natural procrastination patterns. You'll want a plan B and a plan C, rather than being overly dependent and overly insistent on plan A. You'll want safety nets in your life so that falling isn't so awful. And you'll need a positive self-statement that will give you the ability to recover from any mistake or loss by saying to yourself: *"Whatever happens I will survive. I will find a way to carry on. I will not let this be the end of the world for me. I will find a way to lessen the pain in my life and maximize the joy."*

In order to maximize your performance in a stressful world, you must create a protected and indisputable sense of worth for yourself. Until you do, energy and concentration will be drained from work and put into preparing for imagined threats to your survival, and into procrastination as a means of coping. Regardless of how you do it, or what you say, provide a safe place where you make yourself free of judgment, a place and a time where you can stop trying to perform.

If you are threatening yourself with self-hatred and a life of unhappiness unless you achieve your goal, it's impossible to concentrate on work. You must have some sort of protection from these self-imposed threats. Your healthy survival response (commonly thought of as stress) will not stop until you are safe. You need a commitment to yourself and your innate worth that lets you know that, in spite of any failures, you believe in yourself enough to try again, to get back on this board—or some other board more suited to your unique talents.

It's interesting to note how many times successful people suffer through catastrophes and bankruptcies. The successful person fails many times and bounces back; but the failure fails only once, letting that one failure become a judgment of his worth, and thus his label. Following the example of most successful people, you could fall many times, repeatedly using your net to bounce back in order to work for another success. Failure and mistakes then cannot stop you because they can't take away your inner worth and drive.

No book can teach you self-worth. It can only show you how to act as if you have self-worth. You'll start by replacing your procrastination patterns with the positive habits of a producer. As you become more effective in controlling your work habits and guaranteeing your leisure time, you'll be building self-esteem, but it will not be true self-worth until you can talk to yourself in positive language that heals the self-alienation you've learned over the years.

Luckily, you don't need to be perfectly psychoanalyzed, nor do you need to totally love yourself to benefit from replacing your threatening inner dialogue with nurturing and effective self-talk. You will make significant progress in your ability to work with concentration, serenity, and creativity by creating safety and compassion for your human imperfection with your guarantee to yourself: "Whatever happens, I will survive. I make myself safe." When you start to provide this kind of safety for yourself—even if it's just words at first—you will find yourself calmer as you face any task. You'll be calmer because you have directly taken away the threat to your survival —you've lowered the board so that making a mistake isn't so devastating. You're directly attacking the insidious equation, self-worth = performance, so you will not need to use procrastination as a way of coping with threats to esteem and safety. You're unlearning procrastination by changing how you talk to yourself.

3

How to Talk to Yourself

It is not discipline, willpower, or pressure from others that facilitates adherence to a challenging course of action; but rather the freedom to choose among alternatives, the personal commitment to a mission, and the willingness to take responsibility for the consequences of one's decisions that steel the will and embolden the spirit.

—NEIL A. FIORE
The Road Back to Health

The Now Habit system focuses on language, not because a change in language alone will change procrastination, but because how you talk to yourself represents the attitudes and beliefs that determine how you feel and act. The self-talk of procrastinators often unconsciously suggests and reinforces feelings of victimhood, burden, and resistance to authority. The images and feelings created by such language almost always result in procrastination as an act of assertiveness and rebellion. By learning to challenge and replace your negative internal dialogue, you will free yourself from attitudes about your worth and abilities that are inappropriate for your current age, intellect, and power.

COUNTERPRODUCTIVE MESSAGES

When we speak to ourselves in an authoritarian voice, it indicates that we feel pressure to do something, and that, while one part of us is applying the pressure, another part doesn't want to do it. While it is common practice to try to motivate ourselves with statements such as "I have to do it" or "I should do it," such statements loudly communicate to the mind, "I don't want to do it, but I must force myself to do it for them." The inherent self-alienation and subconscious message of such self-talk leads to procrastination.

Through pressure messages we attempt to motivate ourselves by threats that indicate that the task required of us is unpleasant and one we want to escape. These messages, therefore, evoke anxiety and create a negative reaction to work by the implication that it is something we would not freely choose to do. In addition to being counterproductive, such messages fail to point out the direction toward what you *want, decide,* or *choose* to do.

To heal self-alienation and inner conflict between the authoritarian voice and the rebel, you'll need to learn a language that removes the need for conflict within yourself and with those whom you feel have power over you.

Changing how you talk to yourself is a powerful tool for disengaging from procrastination patterns of hesitation and indecision. Through a language of choice, of commitment, and saying no, you'll learn to direct your energy toward a goal, feeling empowered rather than victimized.

The "Have To's"—Messages of Stress

The ambivalent self-talk of procrastination—"I should do it, but I don't want to. I have to because they're making me do it."—communicates victimhood, resistance, stress, and confusion. Of all the characteristics that separate producers from procrastinators, none is more liberating than the producer's focus on "choice" and "choosing." Messages of "I choose," "I decide," or "I will" direct energy toward a single personal goal with clear responsibility for the outcome.

We often get caught in the trap of talking to ourselves in a self-pitying "have to" way about going to see the dentist, sending cards to friends, paying taxes, working, or facing the boss. These statements confirm the belief that others are making us do something against our will. The effect is to create an image of ourselves as defeated by small tasks in life, overburdened, working *hard,* and without joy. Repeated over and over again, a "have to" statement communicates to your subconscious mind

- I don't want to do it.

- They're making me do it against my will.

- I have to do it or else!—something awful and terrible will happen.

- This is a no-win situation: if I don't do it I'll be punished; if I do it I'll be going against myself.

These messages create enormous feelings of outside pressure and of being a helpless victim—conditions ripe for the defensive use of procrastination. Given your healthy need to protect yourself, there will inevitably be ambivalence, resentment, and resistance to tasks that commence with "I have to."

Attempting to deal with all the messages implicit in "I have to," your brain must simultaneously tackle two conflicting situations: providing the energy needed for the imposed task, and providing the energy to resist threats to the integrity of the self—threats to survival. And your body, being a faithful servant, reacts to this "damned if I do, damned if I don't" message with either the stress response (by providing high energy for "fight or flight") or the depressive response (by conserving energy for survival). But your energy can't go in two directions at once, nor can your mind focus on two problems. While you decide whether this is an issue of fighting for your freedom or one of tackling a job, your mind and body are caught in procrastination caused by ambivalent and conflicting messages.

With the confusion of the "have to" message, you're stuck—mentally, physically, and emotionally. Attempting to resolve being stuck by adding pressure through discipline or specters of terrible catastrophes will only make matters worse. These things only confirm the impression that the task is awful and painful—one you wouldn't do if you had a free choice. This feeling is similar to what it was like when, as a child, you were told by those who controlled your food, shelter, and self-image that you had to do something you didn't want to do. All of us know the feeling of ambivalence, pressure, and threat, and the resentment and resistance that go with them. Yet we continue to talk to ourselves as if part of us is like that child who must respond to another part that speaks in the tone of the threatening parent.

When I first met with Betty we needed to act fast. The annual report was already overdue and she was quite depressed and thinking about quitting her job. While Betty was very competent in her job as administrator for a large insurance company, she hated doing the annual report. Each year she would waste considerable time before deciding when she would start. For weeks she could be heard complaining, "I *have to* do the annual report." "I *should* be working on the annual report." "I want to go out to lunch with you, but I *have to* complete the annual report." It was clear to everyone that Betty felt like a victim of something she hated doing. Whenever the annual report was due, her usual energy and cheerfulness would be replaced by a depressed and haggard look. Her back would become bent as if under a great burden and she would suffer from considerable fatigue, muscle tension, and insomnia. Life appeared to be one large "have to" without freedom or fun.

To get some immediate results and to snap out of her feelings of helplessness and victimhood, Betty needed to change her attitude while in the very situation where she was most likely to procrastinate. "As far as I am concerned," I told her, "you don't have to do anything to be a worthwhile person. If you're going to do it, however, you might as well choose to do it with full responsibility for the consequences. Your mind and body will be able to cooperate with that message. Every 'I have to' needs to be replaced with an adult decision about how you will begin the project or how you will explain to your boss that you will not do it." She began after that first session to challenge every "I have to" with a decision—a clear choice that she made as a mature adult.

The next day, Betty chose to work on a part of the annual report she hated the least and asked her boss for help with parts she found more difficult. She also promised herself that if she *chose* to do this report it would be her last. Betty has given herself more alternatives in life, and by standing up for the child part of herself, she no longer feels compelled to procrastinate.

Betty applied the power of choice very effectively.

She now feels more in charge of her life. The childlike side of her once felt caught between her need for approval from authorities and her need to express her fear and her power through procrastination. Now, with her own inner support system and the more productive language of choice, Betty is coping with work pressures in an integrated, unambivalent fashion.

The "Should's"—Messages of Depression

For many of us, the blame and guilt of the procrastination pattern is linked with the language of "should's." *Should* for procrastinators has lost its original meaning: "I dislike the way things are, and I'm going to do something about it." Instead it has come to mean "I'm angry and disappointed about the way things are (that is, different than they should be), and I'm going to complain and feel badly."

The self-talk of "should" has the same negative effect as setting counterproductive goals, envying others, and longing for the future. Each creates the following negative, self-critical comparisons:

- Should compares *ideal* vs. *bad reality.*

- Counterproductive goal compares *finished* vs. *bad start.*

- Envy compares *admired* vs. *bad you.*

- Longing for the future compares *bliss* vs. *bad now.*

Repeated throughout your day, "should's" become a counterproductive chant that programs the mind with the negative subliminal message "I'm bad. Where I am is bad. Life is bad. My level of progress is bad. Nothing is the way it should be." Just as the "have to's" will elicit stress, the "should's" will elicit depression. Just count the number of times you think "should" or "shouldn't" within a ten-minute period, and you will have a good estimate of your degree of depression. Most likely you will experience a sense of burden, victimhood, and failure.

I'm not saying that ideals and goals aren't worth striving for. What I am saying is that "should's" create negative comparisons without indicating how to get from where you are to where you think you should be. "Have to's" and "should's" do *not* communicate to the mind and body a clear picture of:

- *what* you *choose* to do

- *when* you *choose* to do it

- *where* you *choose* to start it

As you begin to speak to yourself in a language that focuses on results rather than blame, on choice rather than *have to,* on what *is* rather than what you think *should be,* you will find that your body and mind cooperate by providing a level of positive energy (that is, without stress or anxiety) free from the unnecessary struggles of the past and negative comparisons with the future.

Being an art dealer was a labor of love for Paul. Unfortunately, while he loved art, Paul hated the management and detail side of his business. When it was necessary to make tax reports to the state or to even find a bill of sale, Paul would waste considerable energy endlessly berating himself with "I should've kept better records" and "I should be putting more energy into promotion." Even when he would start to get his records in order he would think, "It's not as good as it should be because I should have started earlier." What once was a labor of love had become an oppressive burden.

For Paul it didn't seem to matter whether he accomplished some work or he just procrastinated, he always had more "should's" to make himself feel miserable. When he came to me, Paul had to learn to let go of the "I should have's" of the past by accepting that those things were now beyond his control. I taught him how to catch the early signs of depression about lost opportunities, reminding himself to say, "Yes, they're in the past. Too bad; nothing I can do now about that. But what can I do now?" He then practiced rapidly turning his attention toward one, small corrective step he could take now. Paul also learned to turn the stuck energy and worry about future "should's" into constructive effort by asking himself, "When is the next time I can start working toward that goal?" By talking to himself in ways that disrupted his old patterns, Paul became very efficient in diverting self-criticism and depression about the impossible toward something constructive that he could accomplish.

To avoid getting stuck in thoughts about the past or the future, you'll want to start changing your language. To become more productive and efficient, you'll want to clearly communicate to yourself what you choose to do, and when and where you will carry out your commitment to start.

THE POWER OF CHOICE

The vital importance of overcoming the double messages and the ambivalent feelings inherent in "have to" and "should" became clear to me while I was a member of the

101st Airborne Division. Though all paratroopers are technically volunteers, I had had a choice of volunteering for Airborne School or facing the high probability of jumping without training during a time when our unit was constantly on alert for every hot spot around the globe.

I made it through the grueling weeks of double-timing in combat boots and doing push-ups and calisthenics in the hot Georgia sun of Fort Benning, "Home of the Airborne," to discover that they actually expected me to jump from a plane flying 150 miles per hour at an elevation of 2,000 feet. Somehow the effort necessary to get through paratrooper training makes you forget what all that preparation is leading to. Surely if I had worried about it I would have suffered from fear of success—the type caused by anticipating that your reward for hard work is even harder work.

I'll never forget that first flight. The door of the plane was opened and we were clearly expected to jump out. In a line in front of me I saw the other young men attempt to deal with this fearsome task with great hesitation. As they approached the door of the plane, many put their hands on the inside, expressing their ambivalence about leaving; they had been instructed to place their hands on the outside in order to push away from the plane. They looked down at the hard ground, and you could see their bodies tense and automatically recoil inside, as if preparing for a failed jump. From this awkward and unsafe position, they either tried to make themselves jump or were kicked out by the sergeant, which are not optimal ways to leave an airplane. Every once in a while, the sound of a terrible thud could be heard inside the plane as a jumper would fail to completely clear the plane and hit his body against the side. Because of a halfhearted exit he had increased his chances that the chute would malfunction and fail to open properly.

Even though I hadn't totally chosen to be in such a crazy situation and my choices were rotten ones, I knew that I was *not* going to be kicked out of that plane. "One way or the other," I told myself, "if I'm going to leave this plane, it will be under my own power. I'm going to maximize my chances of a safe exit." The change in my feelings at that moment was quite dramatic. Stress was replaced with purposeful action; a sense of victimhood was transformed into empowerment.

When it was my turn to approach the open door, everything about me said, "I'm choosing to leave this plane." There was no hesitation, no ambivalence. I intentionally placed my hands on the outside of the door frame to push off and to remove any doubt about trying to stay inside. Instead of looking down, in anticipation of failure, I looked up, in the direction of a cloud I picked as my goal.

Since I was choosing to jump, I focused all my thoughts and behaviors on that act, fending aside any thoughts of not jumping or "having to" jump. I stepped up to the door with a single purpose. At the signal, I took a deep breath, bent my knees, focused on my cloud, and propelled myself through that doorway, safely clearing the plane by at least six feet.

The thrill of that first jump will always be with me, as will the memory of my joyful laughter as I safely touched down without a scratch. But what has become more important to me over the years is the lesson of empowerment that comes from changing a "have to" into a choice.

From Resistance to Commitment

Limited options and unpleasant choices abound in life. Recovering from an illness, for example, is a common situation in which people can exercise choice. While illness has little to recommend it, it does give us the opportunity to discover that all our monumental "have to's" somehow get done without us, or are survived even when left undone. It also gives us the opportunity as we convalesce to watch, often with great surprise, the sprouting of an authentic *desire* to return to work. Suddenly, we find ourselves choosing to do what formerly we perceived as an onerous imposition.

One can easily imagine the ailing procrastinator in the "bargaining with God" stage of illness praying, "I promise I'll never procrastinate or complain about work again. Just let me get over this illness so I can peacefully, joyfully, and healthfully do my work." To experience that change in energy and attitude about work is truly remarkable and a wonderful gift.

Dieters and people who wish to quit smoking often experience a rapid shift from resistance to commitment when faced with a life-threatening situation or with pregnancy. *The Washington Post* recently carried a story about Gina, who was pregnant with her first child. She had been *trying* to stop smoking and *trying* to improve her diet for years. When Gina got pregnant, "Out went cigarettes and junk food. In came breakfast. Her usual lunch of cashews and a Diet Pepsi was replaced by a sandwich and a glass of milk." She now *wanted* to eat right. It was her personal commitment, her choice, not simply an externally imposed "should."

You don't have to jump out of airplanes, get sick, or become pregnant to experience this powerful change in perspective. In your everyday activities, listen to how images of passivity and powerlessness are created by your negative self-talk: "I have to work through lunch; I have to get gas for the car; I have to buy a gift for my mother; I have to go to the office party." Exercising your power of choice will give you the opportunity to redirect toward constructive effort the energy formerly blocked by feelings of victimhood and resistance.

Are you willing to live with the consequences of not doing these things? How much freer would you feel if you made a clear decision about any of these tasks? You do have a choice. You don't have to *want* to do the task, nor do you have to love it. But if you prefer it to the consequences of not doing it, you can decide to *commit* to it wholeheartedly. Once *you* decide you're going to the office party, the gas station, or the gift shop, it makes sense for you to assert more positively and powerfully (like the powerful adult you are) that "I *am going* to the store; I *will be* at the dentist's at 3:00 P.M.; I *am going* to traffic court this morning."

Since you have made a mature commitment to the task, rather than arguing against it, you might as well be self-nurturing enough to make it as pleasant as possible. Even when the choices are rotten ones, you can exercise your power of choice and learn to embrace the path that makes the most sense to you. And precisely because you have chosen to do it, it becomes less difficult, less painful, and more quickly accomplished. Whenever you catch yourself losing motivation on a project, look for the implicit "have to" in your thinking and make a decision at that moment to embrace the path—as it is, not the way you think it should be—or let go of it. It's your choice.

Learning How to Say No

Children during their "terrible two's" learn to say no to almost everything. This is part of their cognitive and personality development—the development of a self separate from parents. It might also be thought of as an assertion of innate worth, a concise way of saying, "No, I don't have to do it. I don't have to do anything in order to prove that I'm lovable and deserving." Wouldn't it be wonderful to have that kind of certainty about one's worth as an adult? For many adults the only time they can say "No, I don't have to" is when they are sick and can apologetically offer a weak "Sorry, I can't. But as soon as I'm able to sit up and take nourishment I'll be out there slaving away, trying to do what I have to even if it means endangering my health once again."

Saying no is an important practice for procrastinators. It lessens the likelihood that you'll rush into a task in order to make up for a perceived lack of worth. A direct and maturely stated "No" clears the air much more quickly than a passive "Yes, I guess I have to" that you then resent and rebel against by procrastinating.

For procrastinators especially, the ability to say no is a powerful tool for exercising choice. Saying no is another way of saying "I may be imperfect, but I have enough self-respect to say, 'No, I don't have to.'" It's also one way to avoid taking on too much and feeling overwhelmed. It's a way of asserting "I know you can pressure me, but you cannot threaten my sense of worth." "No" can be used assertively and nondefensively, as in:

- "No, I'll need time to think about that."

- "No, I am not as quick as you, and I want time to give it the thoughtful consideration it deserves."

- "No, I would rather have a contract with terms I know I can wholeheartedly embrace than endanger the quality of my work by compromising."

- "No, I will not be paying that bill now, and I'm willing to pay for the privilege by incurring your interest charges."

Developing fresh alternative self-statements that involve choice, commitment, and the ability to say no is an essential step toward having a greater range of possibilities in working on any task and in changing from a procrastinator to an effective producer. You'll find that the following system for reprogramming negative self-statements will quickly get you started linking your old habits to automatic correction in the positive direction of producers.

FIVE SELF-STATEMENTS THAT DISTINGUISH PROCRASTINATORS FROM PRODUCERS

After years of study and a thorough examination of my own procrastination and that of my patients, I have identified five essential negative attitudes or self-statements that lead to procrastination and distinguish procrastinators from producers. While not every symptom will match exactly your own procrastination pattern, identifying which of the five negative statements you use will help you to replace it with positive challenges I've developed.

1. Negative Thinking of "I have to."

Repeated throughout your day, the phrase "I have to" (meaning "I have to, but I don't want to") will give you a sense of ambivalence and victimization ("I have to, but if I were powerful I wouldn't") that justifies procrastination. Having identified this self-statement and the attitude of victimhood that underlies it, you'll want to quickly challenge it with a statement of choice and an attitude of empowerment.

Replace "I have to" with "I choose to."

The language, attitudes, and behaviors of producers can be acquired through specific, on-the-job practice. For example, if you're at your desk looking at a pile of unanswered mail and a list of unreturned telephone calls, the first thing you may notice is that your shoulders begin to droop forward in a depressed, burdened fashion. This is a clear signal that, even if you haven't heard yourself say "I have to," you feel victimized rather than responsible and powerful. At that moment of awareness, immediately *choose* to work or accept responsibility for choosing to delay. Use your awareness of a negative thought or attitude to reflexively shift you to the producer's attitude of choice and power.

2. Negative Thinking of "I must finish."

Telling yourself "I must finish" keeps you focused on the completed product somewhere in the future, without ever telling you where to start. "Finishing" is in the vague distance, a long way from where you may be now in terms of skills, confidence, and perspective. This focus will make the task seem even more overwhelming, almost impossible. It needs to be challenged and replaced with a solid commitment to starting now.

Replace "I must finish" with "When can I start?"

"When can I start" is the catchphrase of the producer. It automatically follows any worries about finishing and being overwhelmed, and replaces their agitated energy with clear focus on what can be tackled now. It works like a feedback device that pushes any wavering focus back to the starting point of the project. And when it is impossible to start now, "When is the next time I can start?" works to preprogram you for a directed and easy start-up in the near future, with a clear picture of when, where, and on what you will be starting.

3. Negative Thinking of "This is so big."

The feeling of being overwhelmed is made worse by thinking of a project as large and important. What you are really saying is, "I don't see how I can tackle such a huge task. This is very important. This project has to impress everyone. This is my one big chance in life."

The bigger and more overwhelming the project seems to you, the greater your tendency to procrastinate. Anxiety will replace the natural tendency toward motivation and curiosity as you overwhelm yourself with all the steps involved and the image of all that's at stake on this one important project.

> **Replace "This is so big" with**
> **"I can take one small step."**

Whenever you begin to feel overwhelmed by the large, grand project that looms before you, remind yourself "I can take one small step. One small step; one rough, rough draft; one imperfect sketch; one small hello. That's all I need to do now." You can never build a house all at once. All you can do now is pour the concrete for the foundation; hammer one nail; raise a wall—one small step at a time. You could never write an entire book now; you can only write one chapter, a few pages at a time. A single, small step is something you know you can accomplish now. When this one manageable step is compared with the colossal undertaking, it gives you time to learn, to relax, and to recuperate between a series of small steps. With each step you will have time to appreciate your accomplishments, to gain perspective on your direction, and to recommit to your long-range goals.

4. Negative Thinking of "I must be perfect."

Telling yourself "I must be perfect, I couldn't stand it if I made a mistake" will greatly increase the chances that you'll need procrastination to buffer you against the pain of failure and criticism. It also means that part of your self-talk is centered around condemning any small steps of progress as being insignificant compared with what you think they *should* be. If you demand of yourself a perfect presentation, a project that is beyond criticism, perfect adherence to a diet, or a spotless home, you are setting yourself up for defeat and inevitable self-criticism. The more perfectionist and self-critical you are, the harder it is to start on a project that you already know will never be quite good enough. Holding on to an image of perfection will make you afraid of seeing what your real product will look like, it will keep you from preparing for failure with a plan that helps you bounce back, and it will increase your tendency to abandon your project when confronted with a normal problem in the developmental process. Ironically, being a perfectionist and criticizing yourself about mistakes makes failures more likely and worse.

Replace "I must be perfect" with "I can be human."

Replace demands for perfect work with acceptance of (not resignation to) your human limits. Accept so-called mistakes (really feedback) as part of a natural learning process. You need self-compassion rather than self-criticism to support your courageous efforts at facing the unavoidable risks of doing real, imperfect work rather than dreaming of the perfect, completed project. You'll want to be especially gentle with yourself as you recognize that, as a novice, you must go through awkward first steps before you achieve the assurance of a master. As you learn to expect and accept imperfect early steps on your projects, you'll build in the persistence of a producer, and you'll be better prepared to bounce back because you'll have a safety net of compassion.

For procrastinators blocked by an addiction to perfectionism, I often recommend a direct attack to unlearn this insidious pattern. Try to be imperfect. Intentionally do the first part of your project sloppily (don't show it to your boss yet); do it fast and inadequately. If you work on a computer, try a yellow pad; if you work in ink, try a pencil or a crayon—but do it with human imperfection. Then watch the process of development toward perfection take place as you appreciate the genius in your early steps and commit to the work of polishing the project.

5. Negative Thinking of "I don't have time to play."

Statements such as "I've got to work all weekend," "I can't, I have to finish this project," "I'm busy tonight. I'm working under a deadline" will make you feel the resentment toward your work that comes from long periods of deprivation and isolation. Repeating these kinds of statements creates the feeling of having a life of obligation and demands that cause you to miss the things other people enjoy in life.

> **Replace** "I don't have time to play" with
> **"I must take time to play."**

Insisting on your regular time for exercise, for dinners with friends, for frequent breaks throughout your day, and frequent vacations throughout your year increases the feelings of inner worth and respect for yourself that are at the heart of unlearning the need for procrastination. Knowing that you have something to look forward to in the near future—a firm commitment to recreation and time with friends—lessens the dread of difficult work. The application of these five positive self-statements lessens the pain associated with work while increasing your chances of finding that work itself can be rewarding. In addition, your quality work increases the enjoyment of your proudly earned guilt-free play. And reinforcing small steps with frequent rewards will increase the likelihood of consistent progress.

The counterproductive self-statements of the procrastinator join together into "I have to finish something big and do it perfectly while working hard for long periods of time without time to play." What you need to do is to challenge and reprogram that confusing and counterproductive statement with the powerful focus of a producer:

> **"I choose to start on one small imperfect step**
> **knowing I have plenty of time for play."**

Fortunately, you don't have to wait until you have completely stopped your negative thoughts and self-statements to change your behavior. That will take time. Instead, you can use your awareness of the old pattern to alert you to choose a more effective path. It's as if you are the switchman on the railroad: a locomotive barreling down the track crosses a trigger point that signals you to divert the engine to another track.

Each time you choose to switch your energy from your procrastination self-talk to the language of the producer, you are wiring in a new track of brain cells—a new neural pathway in your brain. After you switch from the old path to the new several times, the new associations will strengthen, becoming easier to initiate, while the old ones will atrophy. Each time you make a conscious decision to create safety for yourself and to speak the language of the producer, you will be unlearning the habits of a procrastinator while strengthening the new healthy habits of a producer.

Memorize the connection from your old self-statements, listed below on the left, to the corrective, productive ones listed on the right.

Procrastinators	Producers
"I have to"	"I choose to"
"I must finish"	"When can I start?"
"This is so big"	"I can take one small step"
"I must be perfect"	"I can be human"
"I don't have time to play"	"I must take time to play"

4

Guilt-Free Play, Quality Work

One of the most tragic things I know about human nature is that all of us tend to put off living. We are all dreaming of some magical rose garden over the horizon—instead of enjoying the roses that are blooming outside our window today.

—DALE CARNEGIE

We all have heard the joke: "I was going to stop procrastinating, but I decided to put it off." One of the most devastating consequences of procrastination is that it leads to putting off living. We often let its insidious cycle prevent us from experiencing the rewards of accomplishment in our work and the full enjoyment of our play.

"Putting off living" is the most tragic form of procrastination we can engage in. Not only does it keep us from completing the really important tasks in life, it lessens our respect for ourselves by keeping us engaged in destructive, delaying tactics such as overeating, excessive TV watching, the investment of time and money in a succession of halfhearted and rapidly abandoned hobbies and schemes.

Attempting to skimp on holidays, rest, and exercise

leads to suppression of the spirit and motivation as life begins to look like all spinach and no dessert. To sustain high levels of motivation and lessen the urge to procrastinate in the face of life's demands for high-level performance, we need guilt-free play to provide us with periods of physical and mental renewal.

It is no coincidence that similar characteristics separate workaholics and long-term procrastinators from producers and peak performers. Dr. Charles Garfield, author of *Peak Performance,* tells us that peak performers surpass workaholics in taking more vacations, being healthier, and accomplishing more of the tasks that make a real difference. Both workaholics and procrastinators tend to:

- See themselves as always burdened by incomplete work. They see themselves as always working, yet undeserving of a rest.

- Think of their lives as "being on hold," with only the faintest hope that someday they will be organized enough or successful enough to enjoy life.

- View human beings as lazy and in need of discipline to create pressure and motivation. Both use negative self-talk and threats, but workaholics respond to this pressure with constant busyness, while procrastinators respond by being overwhelmed and immobilized by the anxiety.

- Maintain negative attitudes toward work. They see work as infinite and insatiable, requiring deprivation and sacrifice, which workaholics are willing to make, often to avoid getting too close to anyone. Procrastinators exaggerate the sacrifice, escaping to halfhearted play out of fear of never being able to play again.

Both workaholics and chronic procrastinators are either working or feeling guilty about not working. Marilyn Machlowitz, in her book *Workaholics: Living with Them, Working with Them,* and Dr. Alan A. McLean, the Medical Director for IBM, in his book *Work Stress,* indicate that many workaholics are in poor physical shape and suffer from stress, Type A behavior, and burnout. Producers, on the other hand, tend to know the importance of play and the importance of enjoying it without guilt.

THE IMPORTANCE OF PLAY

"Once I'm here and on the air, I'm doing what I love. This isn't work."

—JIM GABBERT
OWNER AND PRESIDENT,
TV 20, SAN FRANCISCO

When someone tells you their job really isn't work, they're telling you, "I don't have to force myself to come to work. I've escaped the confines of the archaic definitions of work, play, and human nature. I have my own sense of purpose that helps me combine work and play. *Work* is fun for me; not the hard, arduous task my early training in the work ethic told me it would be. And I am energetic and motivated—not at all lazy, the way I was taught to believe all people are by nature. I don't need anyone to put pressure on me to make me do my work."

From studying the performance styles of achievers, I

have learned how essential guilt-free play is to attaining quality work and minimizing procrastination. A firm commitment to guilt-free play will recharge your batteries, creating renewed motivation, creativity, and energy for all the other areas of your life. Knowing that work will not deprive you of enjoying the good things of life, you can more easily tackle a large task without the fear of having it rule your life. Knowing that work on a large task will be interrupted by commitments to friends, to exercise, and to free time, you can approach the task with less fear of being overwhelmed. Instead of a project being something that is too big to handle, planned, scheduled guilt-free play lets you know that now there'll be breaks and support along the way.

Guilt-free play is based on the seeming paradox that in order to do productive, high-quality work on important projects, you must stop putting off living and engage wholeheartedly in recreation and relaxation. *That's right,* you can be more productive if you play more! And as you put the strategy of guilt-free play to use, you'll learn to *play more and complete more work.*

My first assignment as a new psychologist at the University of California, Berkeley, Counseling Center was as co-leader of a group for graduate students who were procrastinating on their doctoral dissertations. We met weekly to provide support for these students going through the intense, stressful, and often lonely process of completing the largest single project they had ever faced.

I became interested in the differences between those who were taking many years to complete their work and those who were able to conclude their research and writing within two years or less. Surprisingly, intelligence and emotional problems were not the characteristics that distinguished the two groups. The real difference seemed to be that those who took three to nineteen years to complete their dissertations *suffered more*. These long-term procrastinators:

- Saw themselves as always working. They kept themselves busy without producing much.

- Thought of their lives as "being on hold." They had cleared their calenders so they could always be working, while parties, friends, and exercise were for "A.D." (after dissertation).

- Felt that work required deprivation and sacrifice. Work was difficult; they had to give up something.

- Felt guilty if they spent time on recreation or friends. Because they weren't really being productive, they felt guilty taking any time for fun, so their recreation was halfhearted.

Many of them were in poor physical shape, and their homes were generally a battle zone of papers, books, old coffee containers, and dirty laundry. One of these students had a T-shirt that read, "Don't ask me about my dissertation."

On the other hand, those who were making good progress toward finishing in a year were dedicated and committed *to their leisure time*. Their health and recreation were high priorities and an integral part of their overall plan to do good work on the dissertation. They *had to* swim, run, or dance almost every day. They *had to* be with friends for dinner several nights a week. They were truly "re-created"—in the original sense of the word *rec-*

reation—in a way that kept them motivated and interested in returning to their projects for fifteen, twenty, or twenty-five quality hours a week. Their lives were full. They didn't see their work as depriving them of anything; quite the opposite, working intensely and playing intensely went hand in hand with their enjoyment of life. They were living now—not waiting to begin living when their work was completed.

One of the reasons we procrastinate is out of fear that once we start working there'll be no time for play; work will deprive us of play and the enjoyment of life. Guilt-free play offers you a way around this problem by insisting that you plan recreation in your weekly schedule. Making play a priority in your life is part of learning to overcome procrastination.

Adults usually think of play as being separate from learning and work. But play is an essential part of every child's development and learning about work. Through play we learn the physical, mental, and social skills necessary for adult life. With toys and imagination children create scenarios that rehearse them for work, relationships, and conflict. Through play children express difficult feelings, negotiate and renegotiate promises, solve problems, and learn perseverance, absorption in work, and deep concentration. Some of the most essential and complex learning and "work" we ever do is achieved while playing.

British psychoanalyst and pediatrician D. W. Winnicott writes in his book *Playing and Reality* that it is in playing that we build confidence in the reliability of our creativity and our excitement about discovery—the movement from not-knowing to knowing, from lack of control over problems to control and resolution of problems. Furthermore, it is through play that we learn to work alone with deep concentration, having moved safely and gradually through the earlier steps of enjoying play with mother or father, to enjoying play with a toy in their presence, to playing alone with the confidence of being loved.

Adults use these skills learned in childhood to work alone and sit still for hours in front of a computer terminal, a drafting desk, or an accounting ledger. They call upon the mental and physical states of concentration and creativity that were learned decades earlier while playing in the security of the home. Later in life they will need these experiences to face tasks that require persistent problem-solving and the risk of mistakes and rejection.

The child has no motivation problems. A three-year-old will insist on being involved with sweeping the floor or helping with the dishes. It's all play and learning for the child. But that native excitement about learning gets lost through the process of being taught how to conform to social expectations and that there is punishment for not conforming. There's nothing particularly wrong with understanding social expectations; what's so damaging is the insidious manner in which such teaching too often communicates that we are lazy and could be bad procrastinators. As Winston Churchill said, addressing a similar issue, "Personally I'm always ready to learn, although I do not always like being taught."

Being taught that work is unpleasant and that we are lazy leads us to believe that we need the pressure of "have to's" and "should's" to keep us from escaping to play. And the loss of guilt-free play in our lives makes the tasks of life seem more onerous, depriving, and difficult than they need to be. Guilt-free play can revive your early excitement about learning and doing.

THE PULL METHOD
OF SELF-MOTIVATION

When we approach a difficult project, we typically think of tackling it in big chunks that require long periods of work in isolation. But the anticipation of extended isolation from friends and recreation is likely to promote procrastination. The effects of such work habits on your mind and body are similar to the experiences of prisoners in solitary confinement and subjects in sensory deprivation studies, who are wrapped like mummies to minimize sensation. Each of these activities drastically reduces physical movement and visual stimulation, making the mind ripe for any anxiety created by self-criticism and threats of failure.

We are more likely to work productively when we can anticipate pleasure and success rather than isolation and anxiety. Demanding twenty—or even four—hours of tedious work involving confinement and struggle is hardly calculated to get us motivated, especially when there are so many more pleasurable alternatives available. Given the choice between completing your income taxes and seeing an old friend, the odds are strongly in favor of the old friend—unless you have a strategy.

When attempting to motivate yourself to start working on a goal, do you use pressure to push yourself toward the goal with threats, or do you use your attraction to the goal to pull you forward? Unfortunately, most people use a "push method" of motivation and are unaware that there are alternatives.

In any of a variety of sectors, including the military, business, or institutes of learning, we are subjected to threats—the "push method" of motivation—designed to stimulate action through fear. The fact is that the random action produced by punishment or fear is not directed toward a goal, but rather, like procrastination, toward escape from the fear. These punishing tactics often create a paralyzing rather than a motivating effect. Too often this harsh method is used more to exercise authority and control than to achieve positive results. The use of threats by those in authority is an example of how the attempted solution, rather than generating positive motivation for the goal, is counterproductive and contributes to procrastination by creating resistance to authority, fear of failure, and fear of success.

The "push method" of management assumes that humans are basically lazy and that scaring the hell out of them will create motivation. For example:

- Private Jones, if you don't finish peeling that truckload of potatoes by 1700 hours, you'll lose your weekend pass for the next six months.

- This firm needs to generate $200,000 worth of sales this month or we'll all be looking for jobs.

- Unless you increase the number of clients you see each day to at least fifteen, you can find yourself a new job.

- This freshman class had better learn now that you're in for a lot of hard work. By the end of the semester you'll have read this entire shelf of books; and by the time you graduate, this entire wall of books.

The "pull method," on the other hand, assumes that we are naturally inquisitive, and if we are properly rewarded for our efforts we can persevere with even the most difficult of tasks:

- Private Jones, with each basket of potatoes completed you'll be earning another day's leave. If you can finish that truck by 1700 hours, you'll earn an additional weekend pass.

- We need to generate $200,000 worth of sales this month. That means we'll all need to put out some extra effort so we can breath easier next month. I'd like to hear some ideas on what we need to do to increase calls, customer contacts, and closing of sales by at least ten percent.

- This week you'll be learning how to keep your client on the topic and politely complete the contact. Within two weeks you'll be able to comfortably see fifteen clients a day.

- Imagine that, as you read a chapter of one of your textbooks, you are placing it on this empty shelf. Chapter by chapter and book by book, you'll be filling this entire shelf by the end of your first semester. By the time you graduate you'll have read enough books to fill the shelves of this entire wall.

The "pull method" recognizes that *distant* and *indefinite* rewards, such as a *possible* job after four years of training, have very little power to motivate a person to continually face difficult, overwhelming tasks. The promised rewards for hard work have little effect on what we choose to do now. Instead, the more *immediate* and *definite* rewards of life, such as leisure, seeing friends, and eating ice cream, are immediately and definitely followed by tangible pleasures and have, therefore, a higher probability of occurring.

This model of motivation indicates that there's a low chance that you'll start to work on a task whose immediate results are isolation and pain, and whose rewards are uncertain and in the distant future. It also indicates that the chances of choosing this kind of work over leisure activities are even slimmer because leisure is followed by pleasure, and any punishment that might result is uncertain and a long way off. In other words, to control your work habits you must make the periods of work shorter (less painful) and the rewards more frequent and immediate (more pleasurable)—interlacing short periods of work with breaks and rewards.

If, therefore, you are interested in tackling a large task and minimizing procrastination, you must structure the rewards so as to increase the probability that you will start on the task each day. If you are a manager, you would also want to structure the work environment so that employees received gratification from working together and having a common goal, from helping others, and from compliments for progress made each week, as well as from the certainty and the immediacy of the monthly paycheck.

For those of us raised to believe in the Puritan work ethic, it is hard to grasp that humans are motivated more by pleasure than by pain. In fact, even the original Puritans *had to* stop work on the Sabbath. In addition to the religious importance of worshiping on the Sabbath, the holiday served as a day of rest so that they would be "re-created" and able to work harder the following week so as to be even more productive. Our modern word *recreation* comes from this early workaholic principle.

Modern workaholics, while they minimize the importance of play as a method for overcoming procrastination and working more productively, generally can appreciate the great American tradition of "work hard, play hard." The Now Habit system approaches the connection between recreation and productivity more strategically, however, using reverse psychology to alter the concept slightly so it reads "Play hard in order to work more productively."

When I first met Jeff, a thirty-five-year-old college professor, he was feeling frustrated and guilty that he wasn't as dedicated to his profession as he thought he should be. He wanted to read more research articles and publish in one of his profession's journals. But in the last three years, he had failed at countless attempts to complete a single scholarly paper, and he began to think of himself as lazy and as a procrastinator. Initially, he was a good example of how ineffective "push motivation" can be. But Jeff turned out to be an exceptional example of how guilt-free play and "pull motivation" leads to quality work.

Jeff was stuck. He felt guilty about not making a contribution to his field and was feeling pressure from his colleagues to publish. But he was unwilling to make the commitment to the long hours of solitary work that were required to read professional journals and to write.

After talking with Jeff for a short time it became clear that he had tried, with almost no success, to overcome his procrastination by using every method he could think of for pressuring and scaring himself into writing. I had learned the hard way not to compete with such resistance. We needed a whole new strategy, not more of the same pressure and pushing.

So I decided to say something that I knew would shock and yet intrigue a bright guy like Jeff. I counseled him to stop all this self-torture that only leads to frustration and depression. I said, "Take a rest and do something you really love—something you've wanted to do for a long time." After going through a list that included windsurfing, skiing, singing, tap dancing, and music lessons, Jeff settled on acting with a community theater.

He auditioned for a play and was assigned a minor but substantial part. Jeff quickly found himself with a commitment of twenty to thirty hours a week for rehearsals. This meant he had no time to consider, much less feel guilty about, his professional writing for the entire next two months of rehearsal and production.

Jeff enjoyed the entire process of acting so much that he miraculously managed to find over twenty hours a week—and the energy that that required—to meet his commitment to the director and the rest of the cast.

The play was a success, but more importantly for Jeff, it was fun. Getting thoroughly involved in doing that play was like going on a long-dreamed-of vacation. By some definitions he had worked hard; after all, he had put in enough time each week to constitute a part-time job. But Jeff felt rested and satisfied because it was a labor of love that he looked forward to eagerly each day.

In addition, life during those two months had become more than *trying* to work and feeling guilty about failing to reach his goals. Jeff had learned in a very concrete way that he could commit himself to something and find the time to meet that commitment. At the conclusion of all that work on the play, however, Jeff was mildly depressed. He had completed one of his life's goals and that felt great, but it was not something he could continue to do. Jeff learned that it took a lot of commitment, focus, and time to be in a play. That meant sacrificing some of the other activities he enjoyed. He felt an emptiness now that those twenty-plus hours of intense activity and satisfaction were no longer in his week.

Jeff began to realize that, having cleared twenty to thirty hours a week from his schedule for two months, with a little commitment he could find plenty of time to write an article. But first he would need to change his thinking about this large, imposing task. Jeff now knew how important it was to have something in his week that he really loved to do to lessen the sense of burden and deprivation from working on his research project. He changed the task in his mind from being an all-consuming one—requiring all his spare time—to being one that he would work on part-time, ten to twenty hours a week.

Jeff reorganized his schedule to include firm commitments to exercise and friends. This made it clear to him that his periods of work in isolation would have to be short and focused. Equipped with a greater sense of his ability to enjoy life, Jeff returned to the task of starting on his article.

Finding ten hours a week for writing was relatively easy after having cleared twenty hours for rehearsals. Getting started was still rough, but by maintaining a certain momentum through daily periods of work, Jeff quickly saw the article take shape. From there it was simply a matter of persistence as his natural interest in the topic carried him through to completion—pulling him toward a goal he could now see was achieveable.

Jeff found a way to reintegrate writing into his life without making it a burden and without the use of force or threats. He had his first article ready for submission to a journal in a few months. After an initial rejection and some rewriting, the article was accepted for publication by a very prestigious journal.

FROM GUILT-FREE PLAY TO QUALITY WORK

Enjoying guilt-free play is part of a cycle that will lead you to higher levels of quality, creative work. The cycle follows a pattern that usually begins with *guilt-free play*, or at least the scheduling of it. That gives you a sense of freedom about your life that enables you to more easily settle into a short period of *quality work*. Having completed some quality work on your project, your feeling of self-control increases, as does your confidence in your ability to concentrate and to creatively resolve problems. In turn, your capacity to enjoy *quality, guilt-free play* grows. Your deep sense of having earned time away from work enhances your ability to have focused, quality time with friends, which really begins to pay off as you engage in *creative work while playing*. At this stage in the cycle, the seeds of earlier quality work flourish subconsciously into new ideas, breakthroughs, and motivation to return you to the task rested and interested in applying your new solutions. You are now well rested, inspired, and ready for *greater quality work*. Guilt-free, creative play excites you with motivation to return to work. Sitting before your desk or standing on a podium before hundreds of people, you are primed to work in a way that synthesizes the best of your conscious and subconscious processes because you have learned the secret of guilt-free play. In the next chapter we will learn how to apply this principle in a unique application of reverse psychology, the Unschedule.

As you include guilt-free play among your tools for overcoming procrastination, you will find that insights come to you throughout your day. Suddenly you find that playing golf, jogging, reading a novel, or talking to a friend provide rich metaphors for your sales program, for negotiating a contract, for your presentation to the Board of Directors, or for achieving your goal of quitting smoking. "It just occurred to me while walking back from tennis," you tell your spouse, "how the Jones offer could be a great opportunity for our company." This can happen when you are relaxed because, while your conscious mind is focused somewhere else for two hours of guilt-free play, your creative, subconscious mind can provide clear, almost effortless solutions. Thus guilt-free play leads to greater quality work.

Remember the old adage, "If you want a job done quickly give it to the busiest person"? Well, Carlos was the guy you gave things to if you wanted them done quickly. He had always held at least two jobs from the time he was in high school. He had a part-time job for at least fifteen hours a week all the way through college, while finding time to be active in extracurricular activities and to maintain an active social life. By the time Carlos was a senior in college he had been on so many committees, held so many offices, and managed so many benefits that there wasn't room for all of his activities in the yearbook.

Carlos came from a working-class family where work was accepted as a fact of life. He did not waste time holding any grudges against work, whether it was school work, his part-time job, or the work of putting together a weekend trip. His language reflected a sense of purpose—"I'll start work at eight o'clock," "I'm completing the report this afternoon."

But unlike many harried, seemingly overburdened workaholics, Carlos also enjoyed play. He was as committed to his play as he was to his work. Clearly, he had earned it. And when it was time to return to work, Carlos did so without the slightest hesitation because he felt recharged, revitalized, recommitted.

Carlos was a classic example of someone committed to guilt-free play and optimal performance during work. The vitality of his play carried over into his work and he thoroughly enjoyed challenges in both spheres of his life. When he had something to think over, he knew his leisure time would provide an alternative perspective from which to consider his options. Carlos's dedication to recreation and social events provided him with an opportunity to test out or talk over work concepts in a relatively safe environment. Not only was his recreation enjoyable, it was a source of some of his best ideas and most creative solutions.

This emphasis on the importance of play is not meant to deny the need for work and perseverance. It recognizes the importance of work, only it's not the traditional idea of "work." The usual concept of work separates it from play and implies an inner conflict in which work is seen as something you must force yourself to do. The type of work and commitment that is more compatible with the Now Habit is a *commitment to a mission* that focuses your energies and brings about inner harmony, a commitment that comes from a pull *toward* a goal and an excitement about the process of getting there.

Charles Garfield, in *Peak Performance*, writes of the power of commitment and the shared mission of the Apollo moon-shot program:

> What sparked everyone's imagination and harnessed powers few had known they possessed was the realization that they were taking part in a project that would fulfill one of mankind's oldest dreams. They had a *mission*. I saw men and women of average capabilities tap-

ping resources of personal energy and creativity that resulted in extraordinary human accomplishments. I saw their excitement and pride come alive, affecting everyone around them, kindling imaginations with the possibilities that arose from what we were trying to accomplish. One thing became very clear to me—it is not the goal, but the ultimate *mission* that kindles the imagination, motivating us toward ever higher levels of human achievement.

This sense of mission is really the "pull method" of motivation that draws you toward your goal with positive energy, rather than trying to push you by using fear and threats. In this positive work atmosphere, you are more likely to demonstrate extraordinary capabilities and motivation. Regularly scheduled periods of guilt-free play will give you a fresh outlook on work. They will give you the time to experience your own native curiosity and willingness to do good, quality work. Guilt-free play provides the link between work and play, and each improves the quality of the other.

5

Overcoming Blocks to Action

Serenity Prayer: Grant me the serenity to accept the things I cannot change, courage to change the things I can, and wisdom to know the difference.

—REINHOLD NIEBUHR

Stress Prayer: Grant me the stubbornness to struggle against things I cannot change; the inertia to avoid work on my own behaviors and attitudes which I can change; and the foolishness to ignore the differences between external events beyond my control and my own controllable reactions. But most of all, grant me a contempt for my own human imperfection and the limits of human control.

If you've ever suffered pain from harsh criticism—from yourself, parents, teachers, or friends—for doing less than perfect work, or if you've suffered the humiliation of not knowing how to solve a problem that others found easy, you may have developed a phobic response to certain kinds of work. Until you can find tools to cope directly and positively with that response, your fear or phobia will block your ability to take action.

Procrastination, by putting off what you fear, is a phobic response to work associated with worry and anxiety. When it is your sole defense against something you fear, procrastination becomes a difficult habit to unlearn. While both phobias and procrastination also tend to be addictive because they reward you by lowering tension, they can be unlearned.

To cope effectively with these blocks to action, you'll need alternatives to the addictive and counterproductive solution offered you by procrastination. Armed with Now Habit tools, you can unlearn the phobic response of procrastination and learn alternative ways of coping with your fears. By using the tools provided in this chapter—three-dimensional thinking, the work of worrying, and persistent starting—and by providing yourself with a safety net and positive self-talk, you can approach feared tasks in small, do-able steps. In addition, each time you apply a constructive alternative to help you approach a difficult task, you will be unlearning the old pattern and breaking your addiction.

THREE MAJOR BLOCKS

The three major fears that block action and create procrastination are the terror of being overwhelmed, the fear of failure, and the fear of finishing. These three blocks usually interact with each other and escalate any initial fears and stresses. Overcoming any one of the three quickens the destruction of the remaining blocks because you build confidence as you face and live through any fear. Studies have confirmed that as little as thirty seconds of staying with a feared situation—a barking dog, a crowded party, giving a speech—while using positive self-talk is enough to start the process of replacing a phobic response with positive alternatives. Learning to stay with any fear will be much easier when you have weapons and tools that give you alternatives to running away.

To diminish the stresses and anxieties that lead to avoiding large and important tasks, include the following as part of your Now Habit tools:

- three-dimensional thinking and the reverse calendar, to combat the terror of being overwhelmed and fear of starting
- the work of worrying, to tackle fear of failure and the fear of being imperfect
- persistent starting, to tackle fear of finishing and fear of success

TOOL #1:
THREE-DIMENSIONAL THINKING

Tackling any large project requires an overview of its size, length, and breadth so that you can plan the direction you will take and decide where you will start. When you survey the task before you, you will commonly experience a surge of negative energy (stress or anxiety) as your body tries to be in several places at once along the imagined course of your project. It's as if you have your nose up against a skyscraper with the expectation that you have to scale it in one exhausting leap. You've created a two-dimensional picture of your project—all work, all at once, with no time to catch your breath. This picture telescopes the steps involved so that your body responds with energy to work on all the parts—beginning, middle, and finish line—simultaneously.

Being overwhelmed by a large or important task is a form of psychological and physical terror. As an eager and productive new lawyer, Joel found great satisfaction in working on depositions and briefs that he could complete quickly. However, he shied away from more complicated cases. His fear and procrastination began to get in the way of his advancement in the firm. Whenever he was faced with an important or risky case, his physical and emotional reactions were so strong that he felt stuck, unable to do anything. His worrying resulted in insomnia, increasing indecisiveness about small issues, and increased use of coffee and alcohol. He worried about making a mistake, about his ability to handle the case, about how much work he'd have to do to just adequately complete the case, and about his devastation if he failed. As Joel put it:

> I become so intense about the possibility of losing the case that I stop myself from ever starting the necessary preparation. This makes me so anxious I can't decide how I'm going to handle it—how I'll approach the opposition—where's the best place to start. Then I become so frightened that I'll make a mistake on my choice of what to do that I waste additional valuable time. Eventually, my nervousness and procrastination leave me unable to find time to take depositions and meet court dates.

For Joel, and many others like him, the anxiety of being overwhelmed is increased by the expectation that he should be able to start without anxiety, and by the severe self-criticism he directs toward his initial efforts ("How will I ever finish if this is all I can come up with?").

Conquering the feeling of being overwhelmed starts with anticipating that it is natural to experience a certain amount of anxiety as you picture all the work involved in completing a large project. It is important not to misinterpret this as a sign that you can't do it. This normal level of anxiety will not become *overwhelming* unless

1. You insist on knowing the one *right* place to start. The indecision and delay in looking for the one right place keeps you from getting on to the rest of the project. The possibility that there are several adequate starting points escapes you, and instead you feel anxious that the one you've chosen leads to a devastatingly wrong conclusion. You've gotten yourself stuck by thinking in a right-wrong dichotomy— either you do it right the first time or you're wrong. From this perspective each starting point seems as if it's set in cement, dictating the succeeding steps, domino fashion, thus possibly cascading you in the wrong direction.

2. You have not permitted yourself time along the course of your project for learning, building confidence with each step, and asking for help. Your two-dimensional view pressures you to be competent *now* at all required functions. Even though this may be your first project of this type or size, you expect that you should have the confidence at the start to know what to do, all along the way.

3. You're critical of the fact that you're *only* starting when you "should be finished." Each achievement is diminished by being compared with the imagined ideal. The starting point and the path of trial and error have little legitimacy

in comparison to your goal. You have little tolerance or compassion for your current level of imperfection and your current level of struggle. This critical comparison keeps you jumping back and forth between your negative image of yourself at the start and your ideal of yourself at the finish point. You experience overwhelming anxiety as you attempt to deal with how to make the transition.

The Reverse Calendar

When Joel applied three-dimensional thinking to his assignments, he was able to see the entire process, directing his energy toward dividing the project into small, manageable parts. This view lets you mentally spread the work out over the days and weeks ahead, creating your own deadlines for the subdivisions of the project.

When you learn to look at projects this way, you rapidly diffuse the condensed effort and energy of the overwhelmed feeling over the whole period and project. Now, instead of facing a large, looming, impossible task, you're facing only small units that you can see yourself accomplishing.

I call this the reverse calendar. As you picture several smaller deadlines—all within your control—the paralysis caused by trying to complete a large project (with dire consequences if you fail) disappears. With your own personal deadlines stretched into the future, you've taken some control over the work and created some breathing space in between each step. This revised image of your project enables you to use your other tools to focus on the present, where you can start on the first step. That *extra* energy that you needed in your attempt to do it all at once couldn't go to the imagined parts of the project so you experienced it as anxiety and stress. But with your mind focused on the here and now, where work can be started, your body provides the right level of energy to start.

The reverse calendar starts with the ultimate deadline for your project and then moves back, step by step, to the present where you can focus your energy on starting. You will find the reverse calendar extremely useful whenever you face tasks that require work over a long period—painting the house, mounting an advertising campaign, persevering through a weight-loss program. And the reverse calendar should be used *immediately* if you feel overwhelmed. You'll want a reverse calendar to see what you can tackle right now, where you can delegate, and when you'll have a chance to catch your breath.

1. Ultimate deadline: June 1. Have drawings or speech or project on boss's desk by 9:00 A.M. That means

May 28: Make corrections.

May 26: Review materials.

May 23: Secretary's deadline for mailing out reproductions/making slides/collecting data.

May 15: Complete sketches/rewrites/follow-up calls.

May 1: Start on final portion of project.

April 22: Make changes from meeting with boss.

April 21: Meet with boss on direction and progress.

Today, April 15: Make rough sketches; start outline; decide on most relevant market research and consult with experts.

2. Ultimate deadline: January 1 (next year). Complete negotiations for the contract with XYZ, Inc. That means

December 1: Meeting with lawyers and XYZ manager.

November 20: Call XYZ before leaving for ski trip, Nov. 22–27.

November 1: Deliver last segment of draft contract to Jones.
(*Continue to schedule each month until you come back into the present*)

July 1: Meet with our lawyers.

Today, June 15: Contact Jones at XYZ to discuss deadlines and meeting times.

This approach can be applied to each step of the project. Putting together a large company report, for example, can contain steps which in themselves may be overwhelming. But when the work is divided into its various parts and tackled piecemeal, the first section can be started today. Creating a reverse calendar for the project will give you a time line for each step, letting you know how much time you must allocate in each week—for example, twenty hours a week for five weeks.

Regardless of the size of your report or campaign, the reverse calendar will give you a realistic perspective on how much time it takes to complete each step. *You* now have control over the deadlines; there's not just one big deadline imposed from on high. Along with a greater sense of control over your project comes a relief from external pressure and a greater sense of accomplishment as you complete the many subgoals along the way.

When Joel used the reverse calendar and three-dimensional thinking he could see the individual tasks required in preparing his case: doing the legal research, taking depositions, delegating to a law clerk and legal assistant, checking with senior partners. Joel could now see himself diving in on one task he could handle and getting excited about how the process would unfold. The larger the case, the more it became a dynamic, interactive task requiring a variety of skills over a period of transformation, rather than a mountain he needed to scale in one impossible leap.

Since he had been so concerned about making a mistake, Joel used his reverse calendar to alert himself to those points where he might get anxious and head in the wrong direction. He could then use feelings of insecurity and being overwhelmed to remind himself to pause and think or consult with a colleague. In addition to gaining control over his terror of being overwhelmed, Joel achieved more realistic time management by applying three-dimensional thinking. With the steps of his cases clearly spelled out, Joel was able to anticipate some previously unforeseen difficulties in scheduling and to avoid costly errors.

TOOL #2:
THE WORK OF WORRYING

He said, "For this reason I tell you, do not worry about what you will eat, or about your body, what you will wear; for life is more than nourishment

*and the body more than clothes. . . . Who of you
can add one moment to his life's course by
worrying? So, if you cannot bring about that
little, why be anxious about the rest?"*

LUKE 12:22–26

Worrying can warn you of danger and evoke action to
prepare for that danger. Respect your ability to worry as
a means to alert you to potential danger. But the rapid
flow of frightening thoughts characteristic of most counterproductive worrying simply creates more threats—"It
would be awful if that happened. I couldn't stand it. I have
to do well or else." Stopping there, with simply the frightening aspect of worrying, is like screaming *"Danger!"*
without knowing what to do or where to run. In effect,
your scream has caused a lot of disturbance in people but
has not told them what they can *do* to escape the danger.
By alerting yourself to a potential danger without establishing a plan for how you will cope, you have done only
half of the job of worrying. You've left out the positive
"work of worrying"—developing an action plan.

Once a threat is raised it must be dealt with to avoid
stress—that trapped energy that can't be used productively now. Until you reach a solution or cancel the threat,
worrying can operate like a recurrent nightmare that re-
peats a puzzle or problem. Plans, action, and solutions are
required to direct the energy and complete the work of
worrying.

Procrastination is an ineffective way to cope with worrying because it stalls action and simply piles up more
worries. The worry that accompanies procrastination is
usually learned very early in life. Parents and teachers
often use threats and images of disaster to motivate you
to achieve goals *they* have chosen. This belief that vinegar
can motivate better than honey is so prevalent among

those in charge of our schools, factories, and offices that most of us suffer from some form of fear of failure and worry about being unacceptable because of our imperfection.

Familiar examples are the boss who stingily withholds compliments for the work completed while freely criticizing what is unfinished and imperfect ("You'll have to do a lot better than this. . . . There's a lot more to do and I need this as soon as possible") and the parent or teacher who tries to motivate by saying, "So what if you got three A's—explain how you only got a B in math.")

This terrible training—that your work is never good enough—leads to the belief that *you* are never good enough to satisfy a parent or a boss. Feeling ineffectual regardless of how hard you try is very depressing and damaging to your sense of worth. Without an established sense of worth that bounces back from criticism in the face of normal mistakes, it is extremely difficult to step into the work arena, where some failures can be anticipated and where the longed-for praise for hard work and progress is seldom forthcoming. Eventually the risks seem too great to take and attempts at motivation through threats just don't work anymore.

This syndrome is particularly sad when people with talent will not risk trying for fear of being less than number one. At its worst, their perfectionism and fear of failure ("failure" being defined as being less than perfect) cause them to let their own talents atrophy rather than compete and risk being found second-best. A more common solution for individuals raised on threats is to use their own threatening self-talk in an effort to win approval by mimicking their critical mentors. Rather than helping them to face their fears, such threats will only contribute to the procrastination cycle: threatening self-talk leads to anxiety, then to resistance, resulting in procrastination. Procrastination may temporarily lessen the tension of facing a challenging project and the risk of failing, but it cannot help you escape worry.

Breaking through this block to action requires that you go beyond just scaring yourself with images of potential catastrophes. You want to do the work of worrying to direct the energy of worry and panic into plans to remove the threat. This will help you to productively use stress, your healthy survival response, the way it was intended—to protect you by readying you for positive action. Once you've used this energy properly, your brain, reassured of your physical and psychological well-being, can return you to a normal level of energy for productive work.

For ten years Judith, a bright young accountant, suffered from worries about losing her job because of her continual procrastination. Judith continued to push herself to work in an insurance firm which others had left years before because of the cold and pressured atmosphere. After all, she had learned at an early age that she was lazy and inadequate, that there was always more that could be done, and that she needed constant reminding and pressure from those who cared about her reaching her potential.

In Judith's family individual progress was seldom acknowledged unless it compared well with what others were doing. This pressure to be *the best* was constant whether the arena was school, sports, or musical talent. So it did not surprise Judith when her boss turned out to be someone who provided a similar scarcity of praise and an abundance of pressure. From the boss's point of view, Judith's motivation was supposed to come from her salary and the pressure and threats he supplied.

But for Judith, her working conditions only verified

insecurities learned much earlier. She felt that she didn't deserve much, and feared both failure and success: "I might do something wrong, and they'll think I'm dumb. I feel that people are constantly judging me and that I keep coming up short. But I know, if they were to say I'm smart or talented, I'd still feel anxious because then I'd have to be that way all the time."

The constant fear of being criticized or fired kept Judith in stress and poor health most of the time. But it was her procrastination and her fear of doing increasingly poor work that motivated her to seek help. Like most procrastinators, Judith was a good worker. She wasn't lazy. It was the pressure and the fear of failure that began to block her ability to work. As the stress of anticipated criticism for inadequate work increased and the praise dwindled, Judith's motivation and self-confidence began to dry up. More and more she relied on procrastination as a way to escape and to express her resentment.

It didn't take much for Judith to see that her boss's threats and withholding of praise re-created her family environment. And when Judith recognized that her family environment had taught her low self-esteem, victimhood, resistance, and then destructive coping strategies such as procrastination, she was eager to change her current environment. Even before I discussed the work of worrying as a way to reduce her stress, Judith on her own had begun to consider "what if the worst happened." She realized that though it would be extremely embarrassing and difficult for her, she could face being fired and that, in some ways, it would be a welcome relief. In fact, given her timidity and low self-esteem, it was hard to imagine how she would ever be motivated to look for a better job other than by being fired.

But Judith had decided she wanted more. She wanted

to be freely acknowledged for her work and her talents. Judith was determined to find people who could appreciate her for who she was and what she could do, rather than seeking out those who always demanded that she be something different. She no longer wanted to work under conditions that lowered her self-esteem. Having faced the worst that could happen—being fired—Judith had prepared herself with safety nets of compassionate self-talk and concrete alternatives that would help her cope while looking for a new job.

The work of worrying involves a six-step process for facing fears and creating safety. These steps take you beyond "what if" and direct the blocked energy of anxiety toward constructive preparation for potential danger. When you are continually worried about failing on a project or losing a job, ask yourself

1. *What is the worst that could happen?*
I need to acknowledge the most dreaded scenario that could occur and consider how probable it is. But I must not stop with the question, *"What if* this awful thing occurs?" Stopping there will only keep the worry repeating itself until I ask myself, "What would I do if it did occur?"

2. *What would I do if the worst really happened?*
Instead of just saying that it would be awful, I must consider: Where would I get help? What would I do to cope with getting upset and losing control? Then what would I do? And what would I do after that? I must continue to ask myself, "And then what would I do?" until I know that regardless of what happens, I will continue to do my best to carry on. There is no event so terrible that it can stop me.

3. How would I lessen the pain and get on with as much happiness as possible if the worse did occur?

If all else has failed and I find myself confronted with my most dreaded situation, am I prepared to shorten the depression and self-criticism by forgiving myself for being human, vulnerable, and imperfect? How would I return to the task of improving my life regardless of how bad things get? I must remember those strengths I can build on, strengths that have gotten me through situations in the past that seemed impossible at first. What can I learn from my past achievements about coping with adversity, about my hidden talents, about the strengths that reveal themselves just when I need them?

4. What alternatives would I have?

Have I limited my options by insisting on only one perfect job and by being dictatorial about how I think my life should be? What will I have to do to increase the alternatives that are acceptable to me? Which ones would I permit myself to consider? I must get beyond this idea that I will only tolerate life on my terms. I must remember that I have many ways to be happy and successful.

5. What can I do now to lessen the probability of this dreaded event occurring?

Is there anything I have been procrastinating on—a telephone call, a letter, a meeting—that I need to face in order to lessen worry, create safety, and start me working? Having considered the worst that could happen and having prepared myself to cope with even that, I am now ready to tackle the tasks at hand that may increase my chances for success.

6. Is there anything I can do now to increase my chances of achieving my goal?

After you have considered the worst, made plans for how to deal with it if it occurs, and assured yourself that you have alternatives, you can ask yourself, "Is there anything I can do now to increase my chances of achieving my goal?" Having established a sense of safety by knowing that even in the worst imaginable situation you have alternatives, you are ready to do your best without the burden of fear of failure.

By using the work of worrying, creating safety, and using the language of the producer, you are establishing skills for maintaining genuine self-confidence. Most people wish for an illusory confidence that says, "I must know that I will win; I should have a guarantee that nothing will go wrong." This leaves you at a severe disadvantage because you haven't considered "What will I do if something goes wrong?" Trying to control things so they go just as you imagine them takes enormous energy, keeps you blind to what could go wrong, keeps you from planning for a strategic retreat, and drains you of the energy necessary for bouncing back.

True confidence is knowing that whether you're calm or anxious, whether you succeed or fail, you'll do your best and, if necessary, be ready to pick yourself up to carry on and try again. True confidence is the ability to say, "I am prepared for the worst, now I can focus on the work that will lead to the best."

TOOL #3:
PERSISTENT STARTING

After you've learned to overcome the first two blocks to action and have gotten started, you may need to overcome the fear of finishing. Many procrastinators can get started, but through a number of negative self-state-ments and attitudes they trip themselves up and create blocks to finishing. Difficulties with finishing, like fear of success, can involve certain disincentives for completing a project.

Procrastinating on finishing takes more effort than is required to stay with a project all the way through. It is also less rewarding than the satisfaction in completing a project and making room for more fun and new begin-nings. Establishing structures for overcoming blocks and good work habits for follow-through has benefits that far outshine whatever comfort or excitement there is in pro-crastinating on finishing. As Dr. Joan Minninger wrote of learning a structure for remembering, in *Total Recall: How to Boost Your Memory Power:*

> It's less exciting and dramatic than the chaos caused by missed deadlines and lost car keys. But chaos is exhaust-ing and a real time waster. . . . You're probably seeing the work of remembering as drudgery; something to keep you from having fun. Actually it's just the other way around. When you create structures for the chaos in your life you free yourself. You free up your time and emotional energy for the good stuff.

A thirty-year-old science teacher named Laura was finally completing a master's degree that would enhance her salary and her chances of career advancement. Laura's final research project, however, was dragging on for almost a year. The idea of putting the final touches on a project never interested Laura as much as the excite-ment of starting on a new journey of discovery. It took real discipline for her to sit through the grading of student papers, to finish a painting project at home, or to stay with a hobby until she really mastered it. She was so good at getting things started that Laura wasn't sure if she was a real procrastinator. In fact, Laura was a strong starter in every aspect of her life, including jogging. As it turns out, it was her commitment to jogging and the running of a marathon (guilt-free play) that brought home the attitude change and the motivation to complete her master's degree project.

Laura had prepared herself for months to run her first 26-mile marathon and she had done it right, except for learning how to complete the last six to eight miles when most people "hit the wall"—the sensation of having your body stopped cold by an exhausting drain of its energy stores. When, just beyond the nineteenth mile, Laura experienced the pain of her body screaming for nutrients, she knew she had hit her wall. With seven more miles to go, Laura didn't know how she could crawl to the finish line, much less run. But before she could think about quitting, she found herself saying something that later helped her get beyond procrastination and on to finishing her research project: "I'm in pain. It hurts to run and it hurts to just stand here. It hurts to walk and it would hurt to lie down. Regardless of what I do, it hurts, so I might as well run and get it over with as soon as possible."

What Laura realized is that it takes work to procrastinate and it takes work to face your fear of finishing. There's really no escape from some form of work. Why not tackle the work that's going to reap the most long-range benefits? Her decision to continue the marathon despite the pain made it easier for Laura to apply the rest of her Now Habit skills to completing her research. She had identified her tendency to give up just as her efforts approached completion and the time for being judged. By linking this tendency to her negative self-statements Laura was able to challenge them with the positive language of the producer and direct her efforts toward finishing. Laura's marathon served as a useful metaphor for the steps involved in completing her research.

As with most large tasks, there seemed to be innumerable corrections and additional demands. Bouncing back from the frustration and disappointment of computer failures, oversights, and mistakes was difficult. But Laura had an accomplishment to rely on that had also had plenty of difficulties along the way. During the last months of her research Laura remembered that it wasn't quite good enough to be mentally prepared to run only 26 miles. Even that task had been extended to include the additional 385 yards that makes it an official marathon—26 miles, 385 yards. As she limped passed the 26-mile marker, ready to drop her exhausted body on the ground, Laura didn't hear the applause she expected, but simply the urging to do 385 yards more. By literally counting her steps, Laura learned to avoid being overwhelmed by more work and to focus on what she could do, repeating, "I can take one more step."

Identify the counterproductive statements and attitudes that tend to creep into your mind once you've gotten started on your work. Then use your anticipation of these negative self-statements to prepare challenges that take the fear out of finishing and free up your creative energy for the good stuff.

"I need to do more preparation before I can start." Be alert to when preparation becomes procrastination. You get started and feel good about gathering all the information necessary to do the job, but you feel compelled to ask more questions and do more preparation before commit-

ting your own ideas to action. You made a decision to complete the project, but now that you've gotten through the first steps, your incentive to carry through has flagged. This is especially true if you are a perfectionist, because your fear of making a mistake keeps you checking with experts and making long lists of things to consider, effectively keeping you from diving in.

To overcome this tendency, label as procrastination any tendency to run to the boss for advice or to the library for outside solutions or further preparation. "Work on the project" may need to be strictly defined as your own contributions toward completion, rather than preparation or gathering advice from others. Any *legitimate* reasons for further research can be ascertained when you ask for feedback on what you have completed. Remind yourself, as Laura did, that there's no escape from work: there's work involved in doing more preparation; there's work involved in completing the project; and there's work involved in trying to escape through procrastination. *So why not choose the work of taking one more step forward?*

"At this rate I'll never finish." The rate of learning and accomplishment in the beginning of a project is often slower than you're accustomed to. Remember that later on, when you are more familiar with the subject matter and more confident in your new situation, it will go faster. As you climb a mountain you can see further. You will have time and places to rest. Your learning curve can climb very rapidly, especially when you use positive self-statements to keep your attention focused on the task rather than on self-criticism. Use the flow state (see chapter 7) to experience creative solutions to temporary blocks. Create a positive expectation that as you make

progress on your project there will be large jumps in your learning and your ability. You cannot judge your rate of progress by your current ability or knowledge. As you come closer to finishing your project you will see that your confidence and your ability have been transformed.

"I should have started earlier." You got started and you need to appreciate that. The syndrome of the half-empty glass, so common among self-critical perfectionists, keeps you from taking credit for the steps you've accomplished toward your goal. This project may be larger than you initially anticipated. Now that you've gotten started and can see all the work before you, you may need to do a little more three-dimensional thinking to overcome the terror of being overwhelmed. Break the project into sections interspersed with legitimate breaks and planned vacations. Keep your commitment to guilt-free play. This is not the time for criticism and images of deprivation. Make sure you reward every step of progress, regardless of how small.

"There's only more work after this" One of the fears of success is that more will be demanded of you: "If I do this, they'll expect it on a regular basis. I don't know if I can live up to their expectations—or if I want to." The incentive for completing your current project isn't going to be there if you envision "success" as tying you slavishly to future drudgery. Keep this work separate from your *decision* about future projects. Make a commitment to yourself that you will exercise as much choice as possible about future steps. Avoid feelings of "have to" and victimhood about work that isn't even here yet. You'll make that

decision later, when you see how you feel about mastering this step. Keep in mind that they are separate steps; that you are in control of when you will face the next piece of work; and that you will be stronger and wiser after completing your current step.

"It's not working." Self-talk such as "I'm trying, but it's not working. What's wrong?" can indicate perfectionism and a failure to do the work of worrying to develop alternative plans to make this project succeed in spite of difficulties. A certain amount of discomfort is natural in stretching beyond your comfort zone into a new level of skill. Difficulties and negative thoughts are not a sign to give up, but a signal for you to be creative in either resolving the difficulty or going around it. Rather than hoping for a perfect path with no problems, you can maintain a resolute commitment to make things work. As a producer, you are not testing a system to see if it can make your project painless, nor are you looking for the fantasized perfect plan with no problems. You are focusing on the desired results and making *this* path work.

"I only need a little more time." The engineering, sales, or production department is ready to put your work to use but you're begging for more time to polish it and to look for glitches. You do a wonderful job of carrying out your boss's or client's requests, but then won't let them have the finished product until you're sure it's perfect and free of errors. Regardless of how much others may insist that your work is good enough for what they need, you are terrified to let go of it.

You may find it difficult to accept that others do not hold your high standards of quality. In fact, you may feel a little superior about that. After all, they want something completed—and will hold you responsible for meeting a deadline—while you are more committed to quality than to merely finishing on time. Often you wish you had just one more hour to do a really good job, but they want it now. Even though you're trying to do good work you often feel victimized by a system that rewards people for what they accomplish rather than for their potential or genius.

This form of procrastination requires a hard-headed look at the value of real, completed, imperfect work versus late, incomplete, ideal work. While fantasies are always safer and more perfect than reality, those who suffer from this form of perfectionism need to hear that there is no level of human perfection that will put you above criticism and rejection.

You must learn to tolerate the anxiety and risks of finishing even though you know your work isn't perfect. Acknowledge that valuable time is being wasted on polishing in an attempt to ensure perfection. Learn to cope with criticism by taking your ego off the line—that is, by creating safety and separating your worth from your work. Be aware of your tendency to be phobic about showing your real work—the work that can be accomplished within the deadlines. You'll really need to commit to doing something within the time available. Use tools such as the work of worrying to prepare yourself to deal with anticipated criticism and necessary corrections, but get your work out there—out of the fantasy stage and into the real world.

Keep On Starting

The task of finishing has its own qualities of tying things up and polishing, but essentially, all large tasks are completed in a series of starts. Your skills at overcoming the blocks to action will help you finish. Use these strategies and your recognition of negative self-talk to conquer your terror of being overwhelmed, fear of failure, and fear of finishing. Keep on starting, and finishing will take care of itself.

6

The Unschedule

All the greatest and most important problems of life are fundamentally insoluble. . . . [they were] not solved logically in [their] own terms but faded when confronted with a new and stronger life urge.

—CARL JUNG

Let's not kid ourselves, there's no such thing as a life of complete play. Trying to escape work by procrastinating will only increase your anxiety; *only work will diminish your anxiety.* Neither chocolate-chip cookies nor TV will lessen tension about an overwhelming or unpleasant task. Neither procrastination nor playing will take away your anxiety when there is something difficult to face. The only thing that really helps is to *start working.*

But that's exactly the problem, isn't it? You can't seem to get yourself to start working, at least not the way you feel about "work." *Work* has meant deprivation, facing overwhelming tasks, facing insecurities and internal and external pressures for perfection, and forcing yourself to do something you'd rather not.

But what if, based on a simple system, you could learn to face your fears and tolerate your imperfection long enough to complete just a few minutes of quality work, enabling you to enjoy your leisure time without feeling guilty?

The Unschedule asks you to aim at starting for just thirty minutes. That's right. By committing no more than thirty minutes to work each day, you can begin a program that turns you from a procrastinator to a producer.

While thirty minutes may not seem like enough time to accomplish much on a large project, thirty minutes can be all the time in the world to solve a problem when you are intently focused. You will look at your watch and be surprised at how much you've gotten done in a time that normally would seem so short. You can use a kitchen timer or a stopwatch to accurately record these periods of quality work.

The important thing is that *you got started.* When you've overcome inertia, you've gotten yourself beyond the most difficult part. Sometimes "getting started" is enough to get it finished as well. The act of starting reveals the real work you must do, rather than the work of avoiding what has been feared. As you face that fear you see that there is only work, difficult perhaps, but not the multiple worries and anxieties you imagined.

One of my clients, Carolyn, had procrastinated for months over making the necessary arrangements to buy her mother some Chinese cooking utensils. A number of small problems would get in her way, making the task complicated and hard to deal with—it seemed like a long trip, she didn't know where to get off the train, it would be embarrassing having to ask strangers for directions, she wasn't sure of the exact place in Chinatown to shop. One rainy day when she was procrastinating about something else, she decided to just get on the train and ask someone for her stop and trust that she would find her way. Everything unfolded magically from one step to the next. Upon reaching her destination she checked her watch and discovered that it had taken her nine and one-half minutes. *"Nine and a half minutes!"* she said to herself. "I've been procrastinating for months over something that took me nine and a half minutes!"

EVEN PRODUCERS NEED A SYSTEM

I already had some "real world" experiences as a lieutenant in the army, as a production-line supervisor, and as an economic analyst for an oil firm, when I decided to begin graduate school in counseling and psychology. These earlier experiences taught me about working under pressure and getting the job done when others depended on me. They taught me that I could work effectively and efficiently if I chose to. And yet, when I returned to school, I found myself and my fellow psychology students agonizing for days over papers that would eventually take less than two hours to write.

All of these bright, doctoral-level students of human behavior were struggling as if they knew nothing about directing their own thoughts, feelings, and actions. That seemed odd to me. The theories we studied about personality and abnormal behavior weren't of much help. They didn't work very well for normal problems like procrastinating, sticking to New Year's resolutions, getting the laundry done, getting started on a twenty-page paper, or being on time to meet a friend for dinner.

So I began to search for a system that really *worked* at giving me some control over my behavior with difficult, distasteful, or overwhelming tasks. In my search for a practical system, I discovered that B. F. Skinner, the founder of modern behaviorism, had a time clock connected to his chair. Whenever he sat down to work, he "punched in." Whenever he left his chair the clock stopped, as if he were "punching out." This very prolific writer used a time clock! He maintained flow charts that amounted to giving himself a gold star every time he completed a small segment of work! This amazed me. I said to myself, "If B. F. Skinner has to use a system, then so do I."

That's when I began to record every thirty minutes of uninterrupted quality work onto what I called my Unschedule. I used my Unschedule to punch in whenever I started to work and punched out, taking credit for the actual time worked, just the way B. F. Skinner did with his time clock. Afterward, applying the "pull method" of motivation, I would make certain to do something I really enjoyed.

Within a week of using this strategy I began to notice that I was starting work earlier and getting more done when I could look forward to recording my small achievements and then reward them with time for friends, tennis, reading, and just plain fun. That was the start of my system for goal achievement, based on

- guilt-free play
- quality work
- the Unschedule

That early Unschedule kept track of my quality time worked and started me listing beforehand rewards I could look forward to during my breaks. With this system I was able to complete my doctoral dissertation in one year, while working a part-time job. Because the Unschedule gave me a clear picture of how I spent my time, I know that I averaged fifteen concentrated and productive hours of work a week for one year on that dissertation, with plenty of time for skiing, jogging, and socializing with friends.

The Unschedule is a weekly calender of committed recreational activities that divides the week into manageable pieces with breaks, meals, scheduled socializing, and play, plus a record of periods of productive work completed. It provides producers with a prescheduled commitment to guilt-free time for recreation and socializing, plus a realistic look at the actual time available for work. This method of scheduling encourages you to start earlier on your project, because you now realize how little time is really available for work after you deduct daily chores, meetings, commuting, meals, sleep, and leisure. In addition, starting is easier because thirty minutes of work is too little to be intimidating, while it is enough to make a good start and to receive a break or reward. Thirty minutes reduces work to small, manageable, rewardable chunks that lessen the likelihood that you will feel overwhelmed by the complexity and length of large or menacing projects.

The Unschedule integrates several well-recognized behavioral and psychological principles in an innovative way to address the common problems of procrastination and enable procrastinators to enhance their productivity and creativity. By starting with the scheduling of recreation, leisure, and quality time with friends, the Unschedule avoids one of the first traps of typical programs to overcome procrastination, which begin with the scheduling of work—generating an immediate image of a life devoid of fun and freedom. Instead, the Unschedule reverses this process, beginning with an image of play and a guarantee of your leisure time.

The Unschedule also builds confidence in two ways. It gives you immediate and frequent rewards following short periods of work, rather than delaying a sense of accomplishment until the task is completed. And the habit of recording each period of work in black and white gives you a visible reward that allows you to see how much concentrated, uninterrupted work you have completed each day and each week. The Unschedule's focus on thirty-minute blocks of work creates a nonthreatening goal that even the most timid procrastinator can tackle without fear. Thirty minutes of steady work is enough to give you a sense of accomplishment without creating the fear of failure that often accompanies longer, less realistic scheduling.

REVERSE PSYCHOLOGY

Among its other strategies, the Unschedule turns our natural resistance to structure and authority—one of the principle causes of procrastination—against itself and enlists it in the cause of productivity. For years you've been telling yourself to work harder on difficult projects, to try to put in more time. The Unschedule and the guilt-free play system help you to put *more time into your leisure* and *more quality into your work.* It tells you to work harder at playing:

- Do not work more than twenty hours a week on this project.
- Do not work more than five hours a day on this project.
- You *must* exercise, play, dance at least one hour a day.

- You *must* take at least one day a week off from any work.

- Aim for only thirty minutes of quality work.

- Work for an imperfect, perfectly human first effort.

- Start small.

This strategy reverses those fears of being overwhelmed and of failure and turns them into powerful tools for developing the Now Habit. Our usual habit is to schedule our work time and to leave our play reasonably unstructured. By requiring you to schedule and stick to recreational time, and to limit your work activity at first to predetermined periods of thirty minutes, *the Unschedule builds up an unconscious desire to work more and play less.*

A client of mine in his late twenties, Alan, seemed to be acting like a toddler in the "terrible two's" or a rebellious teenager. Alan's counterproductive "should's" to himself, in the form of "You have to do this work," produced the inevitable "No, I don't have to" whenever he thought about his doctoral dissertation.

While Alan insisted that *he wanted* to complete his graduate degree—that is, that *he* was in charge—his procrastination demonstrated that unconsciously he was resisting pressure from an outside authority that he felt was trying to force him to do something against his will. Having followed this pattern for years, Alan obviously expected more pressure from me. Instead of falling into that trap and becoming identified with his former authority figures, I said, "You've come to me for help in facing a very large and complex task that will take over a year's hard work. That will be a year with less time to be with friends and to do the things you really enjoy. Well, I won't do it." I told him that it was too hard to try to make someone do something he really didn't want to do, and what was more, I didn't blame him a bit. As far as I was concerned, *he didn't have to do it.* "You're perfectly okay just the way you are," I assured him. "There are plenty of people in this world without a Ph.D. after their names who are wonderfully happy and successful. You don't have to do it."

This novel idea got Alan's attention. As soon as it was suggested that he didn't have to undertake the monumental task of putting two to three years' worth of research and writing into a dissertation, Alan began to realize that, if he was not overjoyed at the prospect of all that hard work, he was also unwilling to give up the idea of trying it. However, I wasn't totally convinced that Alan was fully committed. So I told Alan that I would work with him only if he promised to do exactly as I said. *"Do not work more than twenty hours a week,"* I insisted. "And never work more than five hours in any day on your project. Promise me that you will resist the urge to work more than twenty hours a week."

This was another shock for Alan. He hadn't done more than five quality hours *in a week* over the last four years, and here I was telling him that he must promise to work less than five hours *a day.* This created a surprising reversal of pressures.

When I finished my demands Alan was quite angry with me, and after coming out of his shock he said, "Who are you to tell me not to work more than twenty hours a week and less than five hours a day? It's my dissertation." To which I replied, "Yes, it's your dissertation, and you are in charge of how much you *choose* to work, but I would like you to try to resist the urge to do more than twenty hours of work next week."

Alan had been resisting the authorities, the "have to's" and the "should's," by procrastinating. Now to rebel against this new authority he would have to do *more* work, and demand the right to work in excess of the limit I had given him.

The following week Alan returned to my office with his Unschedule filled in. For the first time in four years he had thoroughly enjoyed his leisure activities without guilt. But he had mixed feelings about showing me the number of hours he had worked. Alan was excited because he had completed eighteen hours of quality work. This was far more than he had accomplished in years.

Alan had overcome his procrastination and the inertia of starting. And he had gotten past the imagined authorities he was so used to fighting. This achievement was truly *his*—not a "have to" from them or from me. He was proud of his progress and excited about the remarkable change in his feelings and attitude about work.

But Alan didn't really sense the power of positive resistance and personal accomplishment until several weeks later, when he was able to defy me even further by displaying an Unschedule with twenty-two quality hours completed in one week and six quality hours in one day.

Now, that is a productive use of resistance to authority and your right to insist: "No, I don't have to do it for anybody. I'm perfectly all right just the way I am."

HOW TO USE THE UNSCHEDULE

The guidelines for filling in your own Unschedule have been developed over the past fifteen years with input from thousands of clients and workshop participants. The guidelines have been carefully thought out and I strongly suggest that you follow them for at least two weeks before making any adjustments. Should you choose to experiment with an altered form of the Unschedule, you will find the section "Adjusting Your Unschedule" helpful.

1. Schedule only:

- previously committed time such as meals, sleep, meetings
- free time, recreation, leisure reading
- socializing
- health activities such as swimming, running, tennis
- routine structured events such as commuting time, classes, medical appointments

It is basic to the principles of unscheduling that first you fill in your Unschedule with as many nonwork activities as possible. This will help you overcome the fantasy that you have twenty-four hours a day and forty-eight hours on the weekends to work on your projects. It will sharpen your perception of the actual time available and make you a better manager of your time.

Do *not* schedule work on projects. Remember, first and foremost that the Unschedule guarantees your guilt-free play and the legitimacy of your personal time. This first step will help you avoid scaring yourself with overly ambitious, overly dictatorial plans for work that lead only to failure, disappointment, and self-criticism.

2. Fill in your Unschedule with work on projects only *after* you have completed at least one-half hour. Think of

the Unschedule as a time clock that you punch in as you start work and punch out when you take credit for your progress. You want to maintain an excitement about what has been accomplished, rather than anxiety about how much more there is to do.

3. Take credit *only* for periods of work that represent at least thirty minutes of *uninterrupted* work. Do not record the time on your Unschedule if you stop before thirty minutes are up. The discipline of staying with the task through the first few minutes of potential distractions and inertia is necessary to carry you through to involvement and interest in your work. When you stay with the discipline of *uninterrupted* work, you really know that the half hour you earned on your Unschedule represents *quality work,* not trips to get potato chips or calls to a friend. This mounting achievement will build your pride and confidence in yourself as a producer.

4. Reward yourself with a break or a change to a more enjoyable task after each period worked. You deserve it. You got started! And by overcoming inertia, you have begun to build momentum that will make it easier to get started next time. By rewarding yourself this way for each positive achievement, you are creating positive associations with your work instead of negative ones, creating a new and better habit—the Now Habit.

5. Keep track of the number of quality hours worked each day and each week. Total them up. Emphasize what you *did* accomplish. This is rewarding in itself and establishes a positive pattern by following work with a pat on the back. It also alerts you to those days where you may want to start earlier on your high-priority projects to increase the number of hours worked on a particular day.

6. Always leave at least one full day a week for recreation and any small chores you wish to take care of. Avoid the feeling of resentment and the burnout that can come when there are no holidays because of work. Include family rituals of recreation and play in each week. You will feel more motivated to return to your high-priority projects after resting. Work will be less of a burden when you are experiencing the better parts of life *now,* and your life is not on hold because of work. Take time for yourself and those low-priority chores that you might actually enjoy as a change of pace—repairs around the house, gardening, or letters that you've put off writing. This day is essential for rejuvenation and maintaining creativity and motivation.

7. Before deciding to go to a recreational activity or social commitment, take time out for just thirty minutes of work on your project. Any pleasurable or frequent activity you engage in has the power to create motivation for the activity it follows. By using this "Grandma's Principle"— your ice cream always comes *after* you eat your spinach —you can get started with less pain and foster the creation of good habits.

Soon you'll find that work that previously was difficult or unpleasant is easier and more enjoyable. This technique can even become a springboard for getting started on avoided projects. It (1) uses your attraction to the pleasurable activity to get you started more often; (2) allows you to enjoy the leisure activity without guilt; and (3) starts your subconscious mind working on the project while you play, creatively resolving blocks while your attention is elsewhere, increasing your eagerness to return to the task with your newfound solutions.

8. Focus on starting. Your task is to get to the starting place on time. The advantage of this is that your "to do" list needs only one A-priority item—"When is the next time I can start?" Replace all thoughts about *finishing* with thoughts about when, where, and on what you can *start*.

9. Think small. Do *not* aim to finish a book, write letters, complete your income tax, or to work continuously for even four hours. Aim for *thirty minutes of quality, focused work*.

10. Keep starting. Finishing will take care of itself. When it is time to start the last thirty minutes that will finish the project, that too will be an act of starting—the start of the conclusion of your current project, as well as the beginning of your next. So forget about finishing. If you must worry, worry about starting. In order to finish, that's all you have to do. Keep on starting.

11. Never end down. That is, never stop work when you're blocked or at the end of a section. Remember the "Grandma's Principle": to create good habits you must have your breaks following work. To avoid creating poor work habits, never take a break (a reward) when you're at the end of a segment or when you're ready to give up. Always stay with a tough spot for another five or ten minutes, trying to come up with at least a partial solution that you can pursue later. Remain open and curious about how your mind will rapidly and creatively solve the problem. You'll find that staying with a difficulty for a few more moments is often enough for your brain to creatively resolve it. Gently pushing through a block or starting on the next section before you quit creates positive momentum, making it much easier to get started next time, thus eliminating the need to procrastinate.

Make copies of the blank, twenty-four-hour schedule on pages 124 and 125 for each week, or place clear plastic over it for repeated use. (You may want to enlarge the schedule on a photocopy machine.) You can also use five-by-eight-inch index cards to make your own blank schedule, or adapt it to whatever schedule format is already in your daily appointment book. Note that I've left you twenty-four hours to schedule work and play. This way you account for every hour, including sleep and meals. You also have plenty of room to adapt the schedule to night shifts and morning or evening work habits. Leave two unused spaces—for example, during sleep time—for totaling the amount of time spent on "quality work" each day and a space for your total for the week.

Pages 126 through 129 are reproductions of the Unschedule used by Fran, the assistant manager we met in chapter 2. Fran's Step One (pages 126 through 127) illustrates how Fran followed the guidelines for filling in the Unschedule at the beginning of the week. She set aside time for lunch, telephone calls, and chores; thus her expectations of what could be accomplished during the week were more realistic. This increased her motivation to make time for the project she was most committed to.

Pages 128 and 129 show Fran's Unschedule at the end of the week. Fran used a highlight marker to block out time actually spent on work. At the end of each day, she could quickly scan the blocked-out areas and total her

The Now Habit Unschedule

Hrs.	Sunday	Monday	Tuesday	Wednesday	Thursday	Friday	Saturday
6-7 A.M.							
7-8							
8-9							
9-10							
10-11							
11-12							
12-1 P.M.							
1-2							
2-3							
3-4							
4-5							
5-6							

Hrs.	Sunday	Monday	Tuesday	Wednesday	Thursday	Friday	Saturday
6-7							
7-8							
8-9							
9-10							
10-11							
11-12							
12-1 A.M.							
1-2							
2-3							
3-4							
4-5							
5-6							
Total							

Fran's Step One

Hrs.	Sunday	Monday	Tuesday	Wednesday	Thursday	Friday	Saturday
6-7 A.M.	SLEEP	← SLEEP →					SLEEP ↓
7-8		← EXERCISE, SHOWER, BREAKFAST →					↓
8-9	SUNDAY PAPER	← COMMUTE →					TENNIS WITH JAN
9-10	BRUNCH	← MAIL, CALLS, STAFF CONTACT →					BRUNCH
10-11	↓	MEET JIM					
11-12				PERSONNEL	PERSONNEL		SHOP
12-1 P.M.	HIKE				LUNCH WITH SUE	LUNCH MEETING	CHORES
1-2		LUNCH	LUNCH	LUNCH		CALLS	
2-3		CALLS	CALLS	CALLS			GARDENING
3-4		← MEETING →			CALLS		↓
4-5							
5-6			STAFF				SHOWER

Hrs.	Sunday	Monday	Tuesday	Wednesday	Thursday	Friday	Saturday
6-7	DINNER	←——— COMMUTE (SHOP) ———→					BOB
7-8		AEROBICS	BOB	AEROBICS	DINNER	AEROBICS	DINNER
8-9	BILLS	←—DINNER	DINNER		SYMPHONY		MOVIE
9-10	PLAN WEEK		↓	SKI CLUB		DINNER WITH ALAN & RUTH	
10-11					→		
11-12						MAIL & BILLS	
12-1 A.M.	←——— SLEEP ———		———→		↑		
1-2						←——SLEEP——→	
2-3							
3-4							
4-5							
5-6							
Total							

Fran's Unschedule

Hrs.	Sunday	Monday	Tuesday	Wednesday	Thursday	Friday	Saturday
6-7 A.M.	SLEEP	← SLEEP →				→	SLEEP
7-8	↓	← EXERCISE, SHOWER, BREAKFAST →				→	↓
8-9	SUNDAY PAPER	← COMMUTE (LAUNDRY, PAPER) →				→	TENNIS WITH JAN
9-10	BRUNCH	← MAIL, CALLS, STAFF CONTACT →				→	BRUNCH
10-11	↓	MEET JIM			PERSONNEL		
11-12	HIKE	CALLS	CALLS / CONSULT	PERSONNEL	CONSULT		SHOP
12-1 P.M.	HIKE		MARKETING LUNCH	CALLS	LUNCH WITH SUE	LUNCH MEETING	CHORES
1-2	HIKE	LUNCH	MEETING	LUNCH		CALLS	LUNCH
2-3	HIKE	CALLS	CALLS				GARDENING
3-4	HIKE	← MEETING →		CONSULT FILE	CALLS		↓
4-5					CONSULT	STAFF	READING
5-6	SHOWER		STAFF				SHOWER

Hrs.	Sunday	Monday	Tuesday	Wednesday	Thursday	Friday	Saturday
6-7	DINNER	←———— COMMUTE (SHOP) ————→				↑	BOB
7-8	T.V.	AEROBICS	BOB	AEROBICS	DINNER	AEROBICS	DINNER
8-9	PAY BILLS	←— DINNER —→			SYMPHONY	DINNER WITH ALAN & RUTH	MOVIE
9-10	PLAN WEEK	T.V.	↓	SKI CLUB			
10-11	READING	BILLS READ			→		
11-12	SLEEP	SLEEP	SLEEP	SLEEP	SLEEP	MAIL & BILLS	SLEEP
12-1 A.M.						T.V.	↓
1-2						SLEEP	
2-3							
3-4							
4-5 WORK	.5, .5	.75, 1.0, .5,	1.0, 1.5, .5	.75, 1.0, .75	.5, 1.25,	.5, 1.0,	—
5-6 SUBTOTALS		.75, .5		1.5	.75, 1.0	1.0, .75	WEEK'S TOTAL:
Total	1 hour	3½ hours	3 hours	4 hours	3½ hours	3¼ hours	18¼ hours

work hours. On Saturday Fran indulged in an entire day of guilt-free play.

It's a good idea to use different colors for different activities. For example, if your goal is to include more leisure time in your life, use red for your fun activities. Then you can quickly go through last month's or last year's Unschedules and see how much red (fun) there is in your life. Use your favorite color for your big projects and goals so that you really enjoy filling in the half-hours. Pick a specific color for classes (green), another for meetings (blue), another for socializing with friends (yellow) so that you can quickly locate when that activity is scheduled.

Color-coding the Unschedule will also allow you to quickly spot important patterns in your activities and commitments. You might notice that Fran's Unschedule on Tuesday reveals an extended lunch meeting with the marketing department and some unexpected staff problems, making Tuesday her least productive day. Before Fran applies the old try-harder solution, she might observe that on Tuesdays her Unschedule is lacking in red, yellow, and blue—it's too unstructured. She might need to schedule more time for personnel issues and meetings on Tuesdays so she can lower her expectations about how many hours of quality work could reasonably be achieved on that day. And she may need to schedule more leisure time so she can have something to look forward to and can avoid feeling overwhelmed by seeing nothing but work on the schedule all day long.

After using the Unschedule for two or three weeks, notice the times at which you work best and those days for which you'll need to focus on starting earlier. Mondays, for example, may be your low day of the week, consistently totaling less than three hours of work on your project when your goal is to average four hours a day. As you examine the activities recorded on your Unschedule for Mondays, you might discover that other events take legitimate time from your day, reducing the possible hours available for your project. You might, therefore, need to lower your goals for Mondays. More likely, however, you will find that on Mondays a procrastination pattern (such as being overwhelmed or imagining that you have all day to work on a project) is keeping you from getting started as early as you want. Your Unschedules for the past few weeks will reveal when in your day you were distracted, and your procrastination log will indicate your mood and self-talk at that time. With some awareness and resolve you can be prepared for next Monday, focusing your energies on starting—for thirty minutes—earlier in the day.

A common pattern is a slump following a period of intense work. You might observe that after several eight-hour days of uninterrupted quality work with no breaks on the weekend, you lose a whole week to procrastination or illness. Once in a while you might be able to work this way to meet a deadline, but if you're working on a long-term project you'll need the strategy of a marathoner, not a sprinter. If you are to maintain long-term productivity you'll need to stick to your commitment to scheduled guilt-free play and avoid any workaholic tendencies.

ADJUSTING YOUR UNSCHEDULE

Within two weeks of using the Unschedule you can expect a broader awareness of your work patterns—their strengths and weaknesses—and of how you're spending your time. For example, you will most likely observe that as you structure more leisure activities into your schedule, these cases of relaxation lessen the terror of being over-whelmed by large work projects. You'll find that pre-scheduled breaks and commitments to lunch and exercise help you to use three-dimensional thinking so that you are more confident in your ability to tackle important pro-jects in manageable parts, interspersed with adequate time to catch your breath.

Over the years, I've found that there are a number of discoveries everyone seems to make when they begin to use the Unschedule:

You're probably busier than you thought. Recording your nonwork activities lets you estimate how much time is really available for the projects that make a difference in your career and your life. With all of the demands on your time, you'll need determination to start as early as possible each morning on your special project. You may need to set your own priorities, be more discriminating about urgent vs. important tasks, drop or delegate some projects, and make more hours available for your primary goal.

Certain days are less productive than others. Make note of which days you're losing time to activities such as watching TV or unscheduled visitors to your office. Be especially alert to distractions on those days; reaffirm your commitment to getting past the coffee cart and around the in-basket to your desk for at least thirty minutes first thing in the morning, to start the day with positive mo-mentum.

Other days are so busy that you need to lower your expec-tations about getting started on a big project. Medical emergencies, demands from friends, and unexpected jobs may consume the entire day. You may need to fight off pressure from others just to find ten to thirty minutes to work on *your* important project. (Remember, your priorities, career, and development are worthwhile and deserve your commitment and support.)

Even a half-hour of work on your project is enough to maintain momentum and avoid the extra burden of having to overcome inertia tomorrow. But if this fails, make a strategic retreat to regroup your energies for tomorrow and *freely* choose to spend the time on the other activities. Freeing yourself of guilt will make you even more eager and determined to start the next day.

Beware if after a few weeks you find that you have stopped filling in your leisure time on the Unschedule and are simply recording periods of quality work. This may work fine when you're really cooking on a project, but later you won't have an accurate record of unexpected interruptions. You won't know what's keeping you from being even more efficient or from starting earlier on your projects. Without a record of your legitimate commitments to leisure, you're more apt to feel guilty about lost time or to feel depressed when you see blank spaces on your schedule and can't remember how you spent the time. Make an effort to become more aware of your leisure activities and to record them. Fill in committed times (sleep, meals, commuting, exercise, socializing) and *really commit to them.*

You may prefer to have a consistent time at which to start each day. This can make it easier to create a healthy habit. Schedule a specific *half-hour* for starting on your major project as early as possible in your day. You might set aside a half-hour every morning for starting on your

AAA-priority project. When this is done you are free to aim for starting on your next-highest priority during the *next* possible half-hour. Fill in the quality time worked only when you've completed it; then take credit for it by adding it to your total for the day.

Use your most frequent, "high-occurrence" behaviors (generally your favorite activities) as motivation tools to increase and reinforce any positive habit you want to strengthen. If, for example, you watch TV after giving up on a project, giving up will become an even stronger habit because it is followed by a reward. Conversely, if balancing the books, writing, or painting comes before watching TV, eating, or sleeping, a positive habit is formed. As these achievements become associated with pleasure, we engage in them more easily and frequently.

You will constantly find new ways to adapt the Unschedule to the specific needs of your work and play situations. Experiment with ideas that personalize it for you: start your week on Saturday or Wednesday, or reduce the blank schedule to fit in your appointment book. The real key to forming your own Now Habit is to adapt its strategies and tools so they fit your personal style.

The Unschedule is meant to help you integrate the Now Habit strategies and tools so you can focus your energies on being a producer. Using the Unschedule provides several benefits that lead to greater enjoyment of guilt-free play and overcoming procrastination.

1. Realistic timekeeping. By first recording all your committed time—such as sleep, meals, exercise, classes, meetings, laundry, and reading—you become acutely aware of how much time is really left for working on your stated goals. This rapidly cures the fantasy of "having all week" and the awful surprise of "I forgot that my parents were visiting." Realistic timekeeping will become a major weapon in your expanding armory for combating procrastination.

2. Thirty minutes of quality time. By aiming at *starting* (rather than finishing) for just thirty minutes, there is a greater likelihood that you won't feel overwhelmed. When you start on a different task one step at a time for short periods, you can achieve a sense of accomplishment sooner that if you set big goals with distant rewards. Every half-hour or fifteen minutes can be used to get something done or at least something organized, so that starting is easier next time. By starting small you will have more opportunities during your day to chip away at the big, long-term goals, participate fully in life, and experience the power of your creative faculty working in the background while you complete other tasks and enjoy your well-deserved recreation.

3. Experiencing success. By recording time worked, you see your progress rather than your failure to meet an unrealistic schedule. By scheduling rewards or alternative activities, you lessen the deprivation associated with work and begin to experience it as something that gives you pride and allows you to enjoy your leisure time.

4. Self-imposed deadlines. Deadlines often create a certain amount of productive pressure, but they're usually too late to allow for quality work. Any student knows the benefits of cramming under the gun of the deadline: studying or writing must be efficient, to the point; work is done with full attention and the excitement of being creative under pressure. The deadline not only clarifies the time frame, it indicates when you will be rewarded for your efforts or punished for your failure to complete the task—only now *you* control the deadline. And with the Unschedule system, the consequence of completing one-half hour or more of quality work is that you get to maintain your commitment to your health, your friends, or other "to-do" list items—*without guilt.* Getting a reward after a short period of work greatly increases your positive associations with work and increases the tendency to return to the work project—that is, it helps you to form a positive habit.

5. Newfound "free time." One of the many fringe benefits of prescheduling your leisure activities is that, when one of them is cancelled, you can suddenly find yourself thinking with relief, "I have free time; I can work." Previously, trying to make yourself work during that time would have been very difficult. But now whenever you unexpectedly find yourself with time on your hands, you'll be reaping the benefits of reverse psychology in the form of scheduled playtime: you'll experience that wonderful and often surprising sense of motivation to get something done. When you've lived as a chronic procrastinator, telling yourself that you're lazy and worthless, it is quite a pleasant shock to discover that you actually *want* to do some work with your newfound free time.

7

Working in the Flow State

New research is leading to the conclusion that these instances of . . . [being fully absorbed in a challenging task] are, in effect, altered states in which the mind functions at its peak, time is often distorted, and a sense of happiness seems to pervade the moment.

—DANIEL GOLEMAN
New York Times

Learning to work creatively and knowing that you can tap into creative states at will can lessen the drudgery of work and increase your excitement about how you work. By decreasing the agony of onerous work, creative states of mind bypass much of the struggle and fear that cause you to defend yourself with procrastination.

We all experience daily shifts of consciousness into natural levels of calm, focused energy, and attention. At these times our ability to concentrate is much improved so we are able to focus on one topic, screening out extraneous stimuli, and are less likely to be distracted by the fears and worries that lead to procrastination. During these special states, our tolerance for noise and pain is higher than usual while the pulse rate, blood pressure, and heart rate are lower, and metabolism is more efficient. It's a healthier state, in which our ability to perform athletic or creative tasks and solve problems increases.

You can learn methods to reach this state and thus work at a genius or near-genius level. This technique, which I call "working in the flow state," will teach you to more readily shift levels of consciousness and brain functions so that you can work with greater energy, enthusiasm, and efficiency.

Rather than waiting until you feel perfect or for the "right mood" to inspire you to work, you can use this technique so that "just do it" becomes a real possibility, instead of hackneyed advice on overcoming procrastination.

In the May 1987 issue of *Esquire* magazine, journalist John Poppy reported on mental states labeled "flow states" by researchers at the University of Chicago and "mindfulness" by those studying states of active attention at Harvard. Characteristics of the flow state include calm, focused energy; time expansion; delight at new ideas; ease at avoiding or solving problems; and enhanced concentration.

Poppy described the flow state of athletes as "reflecting an inner state that is both intensely focused and exceptionally calm. Those we most admire in sports seem at times to enter another dimension. Besieged by opposing players, battered by the screams of the crowd, they make the difficult, even the supernatural, seem easy and . . . create harmony where chaos might otherwise prevail."

Peak performers in sports, music, medicine, and business have these experiences when they are fully absorbed with almost effortless attention in a challenging task. Psychological and physical health benefits, invigoration, and relaxed alertness have been attributed to these states.

Getting into this state of "mental overdrive" on command takes some training, but it can be learned and applied to daily chores around the home and projects at the office.

USING MORE OF YOUR BRAIN

Getting into the flow state as a precondition for work helps you to bridge the gap between the linear and the creative functions of your brain. This process is as natural as the "willing suspension of disbelief" (temporarily putting aside the critical faculty of your logical mind) that lets you enjoy a movie or play without continually being reminded that what's happening is not real. I don't envy the job of film critics who, while trying to get lost in a delightful film, must constantly retrieve their critical faculty to evaluate the lighting, acting, music, and camera angles.

You can tell that your critical functions are getting in the way of your creative side if you hear yourself saying

"But is this the right direction?"

"Will it be good enough?"

"What if the boss/teacher/audience isn't happy with it?"

"Can I do it?"

"I have to finish soon."

"When will I ever learn to start earlier?"

"There's so much to do."

For you to work creatively, and very rapidly, the critical and logical functions of your brain (generally attributed to the left hemisphere) must be temporarily suspended to allow the creative functions (generally attributed to the right hemisphere) to start the flow of ideas and inspiration that you need. Later, the left side can organize them to fit the requirements of the project or customer. The critical/linear function is vital to the creative process in its own way, but if the creative side is to be given a chance to demonstrate what you know at a deeper level—what the larger portion of your brain can do—the critical function must be delayed until after you've established a mental beachhead from which to work. In order for this shift to take place, concerns about perfection, accuracy, and acceptance must be put aside temporarily.

Most of us approach work, exams, and creative tasks as if we are only capable of linear thought and survival functioning (stress)—using only the left hemisphere of the cerebral cortex and the reptilian brain, respectively. The procrastination mind-set, with its threatening images of potential failure and loss of approval, will halt creativity and impede access to the higher, most recently developed functions of the brain, turning the potential joy of the creative process into frustration. Trying to be creative (or to relax and concentrate) can become almost impossible if the so-called practical part of your brain is attempting to supervise, criticize, and fix every possible error before your intuitive side has had a chance to gain confidence at an awkward or unpleasant task.

Yet, if properly used, the creative, right hemisphere of your cerebral cortex in just seconds can provide more than enough ideas and images to fill a book or make a movie. Reached through creative states of mind, this portion of your brain lets ideas flow as if you're dreaming in Technicolor, with Dolby sound and Smellorama—experiencing three-dimensional imagery and input from all your senses. But as soon as you sit down to construct this dream out of words, paint, or wood, you must do it one step at a time, from past to present to future, down the page—without the immediacy, full orchestration, and wraparound sound of your original, uncensored concept.

Trying to cram all the emotion and experience of a spontaneous creative idea into a linear form is one of the major causes of "creative blocks" and procrastination. That's why it's important to know how to use more of your brain and how to shift into the flow state.

IT'S ONLY YOUR FIRST DRAFT

The pleasure of creativity is the greatest pleasure in the world.

—SAMMY KAHN
ACADEMY AWARD–WINNING SONGWRITER

The need to temporarily suspend criticism and linear thought at the start of a project is apparent in most fields, but especially in architecture, the arts, and writing. In occupations that rely heavily on creativity, the early renderings of a project must be protected from overly critical comparison with the ideal and ultimate goal.

The early drafts and sketches of great writers and artists reflect the same nonlinear, seemingly disorganized creative process we all experience when we start a new project. Their initial offerings, like our own, require progressive polishings and reordering before the work reaches its final form. By observing how the geniuses struggle with early versions of their work, we can speed up our progress through the awkward beginning stages of overcoming procrastination and blocks in our work.

Students entering Harvard, for example, are brought to a special section of the library where the rough drafts of famous authors are kept. This exercise has quite an impact on young writers who previously thought that the work of geniuses arrived complete, in a single stroke of inspiration. Here, the freshmen can examine how a successful artist often starts with an apparently random series of ideas centered around a theme; many of these ideas later proved superfluous to the final design, but were essential to the *process* of developing a new concept. That is, the early drafts are not discarded like mistakes, but are viewed as the initial steps in unfolding the idea. The linear ordering of ideas comes later, as a second process, to communicate the original experience in a sequence that can be appreciated. In developing the final, polished version, the last part to be completed is often placed as an introduction or first part of the finished design, and often the initial concepts can only be seen in the conclusion.

LEARNING TO FOCUS

Performing the following focusing exercise each time you start work on your project can help you begin a creative process that will easily evolve into the finished product while you develop positive work habits. Allowing a few moments to shift into a creative, noncritical state of mind is essential for optimal performance and unlearning procrastination habits.

Regardless of how you feel, within two minutes you will be focused, curious, motivated, and creative. And, most important of all, you will have started—and be on your way to finishing.

Focusing is a two-minute procedure for shifting rapidly to the flow state by replacing guilt and stress with a stress-free focus on the present. The relaxation and imagery of this focusing exercise are geared to enhancing your performance at work and your ability to overcome procrastination by creating positive neural patterns to replace negative habit patterns. Although two minutes may seem incredibly short for "a dynamic, miraculous step," in my experience with thousands of clients, that's as long as it takes for anyone with some training in meditation and relaxation techniques.

In *Seven Steps to Peak Performance,* Dr. Richard M. Suinn states that deep relaxation measurably enhances the neuromuscular training of Olympic athletes who use mental imagery for successful performances. If you are new to relaxation techniques, you will gain more from this two-minute procedure after first experiencing profound relaxation through the use of a longer exercise, such as the one on page 148. Whether you are a novice or an expert, periodic (for example, weekly) practice of twenty-minute relaxation exercises is beneficial to remind you of the positive feelings and mental attitude brought about by deeper, longer periods of relaxation.

Within two weeks of daily practice with the focusing exercise, you will be able to achieve an adequate level of relaxation, and most of the benefits of a twenty- to thirty-minute exercise, in just two minutes.

The focusing exercise is purposefully short so that it can be *used* throughout your day and easily accommodated to your busy schedule, rather than requiring a separate time for practice. You can use it in preparing for making calls to difficult clients, between meetings and presentations, for calming down after an upsetting confrontation, and before and after commuting.

This exercise can be read or played back on a tape

recorder until you know it by heart. You will learn to associate sitting at your desk with automatically doing this exercise. Use it each time you begin work and it will quickly lead you beyond pressure and worry about failure into the flow state. This focusing exercise also serves as a good example of the reassuring, present-focused self-talk of the producer.

FOCUSING EXERCISE

Start by sitting upright in your chair with your feet flat on the floor, with your hands on your thighs. Focus your attention on your breathing. If you've been stressed you may discover that your breathing is constricted. Breathe deeply, holding your breath for a moment, and then exhale slowly and completely. Do this three times, counting each time you exhale. With each exhalation imagine that you are letting go of any remaining tension and that you are deciding to drift to a different level of mind.

Now focus your attention on the feeling of the chair against your back, buttocks, and legs. Float down into the chair. Let it support you, as you release any unnecessary muscle tension. You can now let go of those muscles. Shift your attention to the floor, and let it support your feet. Now let go of those muscles. As you let go, continue to exhale away any remaining tension. Just let go and allow your body to give you the gift of relaxation and support.

During the next few moments, there is nothing much for your conscious mind to do except to be curious and allow your subconscious mind to provide your body with deeper and deeper relaxation with each phrase.

Now, notice how heavy your eyelids are beginning to feel. And as you experience them getting heavier and heavier, let them float softly closed over your eyes. Or you can try to keep them open, and find that it takes so much effort to try that it's much more comfortable to let them float down of their own accord. As your eyes close, allow relaxation to flow down over your entire body.

Letting go of the past. With your next three slow, deep breaths, tell yourself to let go of all thoughts and images about work from the past. Let go of what you've just been doing—driving in heavy traffic, making a telephone call, cleaning the house. Let go of thoughts about what you've been telling yourself you should or shouldn't have done. You may even want to let go of your old self-image—your former sense of identity and its limitations on your potential.

Letting go of the future. And with your next three slow, deep breaths, let go of what you anticipate happening in the "future"—a constructed concept of a time that really doesn't exist. Let go of all thoughts and images of future work and deadlines—freeing more energy for focusing in the present.

Centering in the present. With your next three slow, deep breaths, notice—just notice—that it really doesn't take much energy to just *be* in the present. Let go of trying to be in any particular time, and let go of striving to be any particular way. Just allow yourself to notice the sensations of being where you are now. Choose to be in this situation, allowing the wisdom of your body and inner mind to give you the just right level of energy and relaxation to be here, doing whatever you choose to do in this moment.

You can now find yourself at a deeper level of relaxation where you can give yourself any positive suggestion you wish. With your next three slow, deep breaths, you can begin to link the power of the right and left hemispheres of your brain, reaching the flow state under your conscious control.

After taking about a minute to complete the first part in twelve breaths, use any one of the following conclusions to complete your focusing on a specific issue.

To overcome procrastination and stimulate interest in starting work, count up from 1 to 3, and say to yourself:

> With each breath I become more alert, curious, and interested in how rapidly I'll be going beyond discomfort and worry to starting with purpose and commitment in just a few seconds of clock time—1. Becoming more and more alert and ready to begin as I tap into the inner wisdom of my mind and many alternative solutions—2. Coming all the way up to full alertness, operating at a genius level with the support of my entire brain and my creative faculty, ready and eager to begin—3.

This next example of the focusing exercise is useful when you feel stuck and frustrated with the limited abilities of your linear, conscious attempts at solutions. This conclusion is directed toward feeling more comfortable with your initial confusion and lack of confidence. Use it to proceed rapidly beyond critical self-judgment to positive suggestions about accomplishing your task and an intense interest in your own creative way of solving problems.

> With each breath I am tapping into my creative self, opening more and more of my brain power to my task.

My conscious mind may not know yet what to do, just as it doesn't know how a puzzle will look until it's finished. *I* may not know how I'm going to do this, but soon something will come to me and then a little bit more. And I will find that process very interesting, because while I don't know yet what the solution will be, I do know that I will do it and that part of me already knows how to do it. It will also be interesting to see how time feels different at this level of the mind, and to wonder about how much I will accomplish in such a short period of *clock* time.

Counting up from one to three, I am becoming more quietly alert and am now ready to work in a focused, concentrated way, rapidly going from not knowing to knowing how to start—1. More alert, relaxed, and energized, ready to use the superior wisdom of my subconscious mind—2. Ready to come all the way up to full alertness with my eyes open, eager to work in conjunction with the creative faculties of my mind—3.

If you've been procrastinating out of fear of confronting a boss, employee, or loved one, the next version of the exercise will be valuable in getting unstuck from negative patterns of social interaction. Use it to establish your own safety and protection, so that nothing is taken too personally. Then give yourself time to consider the results you wish to achieve and the alternative responses that will get you there. And finally, visualize a positive outcome—that rather than confronting each other as enemies, you and this other person can become valuable allies to each other.

I create the feeling of a warm, golden glow around me, an atmosphere that protects me from any distracting words and attitudes of others, and even from any negative thoughts of my own. I have all the time in the world to consider thoughts and remarks or to push them aside and to return my focus toward positive attitudes and my chosen goals. My thoughts and actions convey to others that I am their ally. Others can only help me. I am becoming more and more robust in my world and can be friendly and generous as I use my inner resources to cope with each challenge and opportunity.

Counting up from one to three, I return to normal wakefulness, bringing with me my own safe, supportive, warm, cocoon of golden light—1. Becoming more and more quietly and peacefully alert—2. Ready to open my eyes and participate fully in a safe and supportive atmosphere—3.

RELAXATION EXERCISE

This exercise can be read into a tape recorder and used on a daily basis to practice speaking in a language your body can cooperate with to bring you relaxation and stillness of mind. The exercise takes twelve to fifteen minutes and is good preparation for the one-to-two-minute focusing exercise.

This exercise is directed toward the warming of your hands: that is, you will be able to dilate your blood vessels and the tiny capillaries of your hands and fingers. You cannot achieve this by commanding it to happen, the way you might command your hand to open. You can only do this by letting go of central nervous system control and allowing your autonomic nervous system to cooperate.

This is *your* exercise. *You* will be *in control* at all times. If you wish to open your eyes or shift your position, you can do so. There is no right or wrong way to achieve relaxation, just *your* way, at whatever rate and to whatever depth is just right for you.

You can start by sitting erect with your feet flat on the floor and with your hands in your lap. Allow your eyelids to float softly closed over your eyes as you turn your attention inward, toward your breathing. Now breathe deeply, hold your breath for a moment, and then exhale slowly and completely. Do this three times, letting your exhalation be a signal that you are letting go of any remaining tension. You can now notice the chair and let it support you, floating down into it; no need for you to hold. You can let go of those muscles; and now focus on how the floor is supporting your feet, and let go of those muscles. No need for you to hold: just let go and allow your body to give you the gift of relaxation and proper support. Now, there is nothing for you to do except to allow your conscious mind to be curious and watch as your body and subconscious mind cooperate with the process of providing you deeper and deeper relaxation with each phrase.

I will state all the phrases in the first person, and you can repeat them silently to yourself in the first person. For example: *I am sitting still.* As you repeat each phrase, you just imagine, visualize, and feel the change happening. And then just let it happen, letting your body carry out the directions you have given it. This is called "passive volition"—by imagining, visualizing, and feeling the direction given in each phrase you are stating your will in a language your body can understand. You are letting the will give direction in a passive way, without using force and without trying to make anything happen.

You quietly let the change happen, using your body's natural tendency to cooperate. And now, you can make yourself comfortable and be ready to proceed, continuing to breathe deeply and slowly, repeating quietly to yourself

I feel quiet. I am beginning to feel quite relaxed—my feet feel quiet and relaxed, my ankles, my knees, and my hips feel light, calm, and comfortable. My stomach and the entire center of my body feels light, calm, and comfortable.

My entire body feels quiet, calm, and comfortable. I feel relaxed. My arms and my hands are quiet and warm. I feel quite quiet. My entire body is calm and my hands are warm—relaxed and warm. My hands feel warm. My hands are warm. My hands are slowly becoming warmer. I can continue to breathe deeply and slowly.

My entire body is quiet, comfortable, and calm. My mind is quiet. I withdraw myself from my surroundings and feel serene and still. My thoughts are turning inward. I feel at ease. Within myself I can visualize and experience myself as calm, comfortable, and quiet. In an easy, quiet, inward-turning way I am quietly alert. My mind is calm and quiet. I feel an inward quietness.

I will continue with these thoughts for two minutes and then softly open my eyes, feeling fine, relaxed, and quietly alert. The next time that I speak, two minutes of clock time will have gone by, and it will be interesting to note how deeply relaxed I can get in a time that is normally so short.

(Allow two minutes to pass.)

Well, fine, and did that feel like two minutes to you? Do you feel as if you've had a nice nap? Want to stretch and discover if your hands are warmer and more relaxed?

Now take three slow, deep breaths and with each

breath become more quietly alert; adequately alert; ready to begin on some project or task in a very relaxed and focused way.

INCORPORATING FLOW STATES INTO YOUR PROGRAM

Working in the flow state removes the emotional need to procrastinate and accelerates your progress toward your goals. The flow state provides a magical bridge from anxiety into tranquillity and safety by teaching you how to rapidly shift from your brain's survival functions to its creative functions. You already know how to talk to yourself with messages of safety and direction that evoke the right level of energy for work. You know how to give yourself clear, resolute statements such as "I will be at my desk at 3:00 P.M. for thirty quality minutes, with great curiosity and interest," "I choose to start at 8:00 A.M. by writing one more letter," "At 10 I will find one file and stay with it for at least fifteen minutes," "I can start on a small part of the budget by 11:30 A.M., and really look forward to lunch."

These statements combine the three elements of effective work imagery (when, where, and on what you will start) and imply *choice, safety,* and *starting.*

The fourth step necessary to complete the process and tap into the power of working in the flow state is one we discussed earlier in this chapter—*focusing.*

A dedicated father and husband with workaholic tendencies, Jacob worried about being able to provide for his family. He was starting out at age forty in a new career that took him beyond his comfort zone of working with his hands to supervision, management, and customer contact. For almost fifteen years he had worked as a carpenter and had just switched to the contracting business when he started having problems with the main causes of procrastination—feeling overwhelmed, fear of failure, and fear of success.

Bringing in customers was no problem for Jacob. His commitment to excellence showed, and his work sold itself. But Jacob was having problems following through on his jobs. His perfectionism had gained him a reputation for doing excellent work, but his clients often had deadlines that didn't allow time for perfection. Jacob was being overwhelmed by his own success. He had difficulty deciding which jobs to pursue, which to turn down, and which to start on immediately. In response to all this new aggravation and feelings of being overwhelmed, Jacob began to avoid telephone messages and to delay acting on client and employee demands.

Among the issues that caused Jacob to become indecisive and to procrastinate were (1) worries about overextending himself; (2) dealing with customer complaints; (3) handling telephone calls; (4) difficulties at the job site; (5) increases in the cost of supplies; (6) worries about finishing on time; (7) cash-flow problems; and (8) dealing with contracts and paperwork.

His background had not prepared Jacob for success. He was the oldest of five children and had watched his parents work hard all their lives, while never getting out from under their debts and financial worries. His father died of a stroke a year before he was to retire. The lesson of his parents' lives was not lost on Jacob. He lived a more secure life than they had ever known, yet he was caught in similar compulsive worrying about financial security, in addition to worrying about his health. Now that he was his own boss he didn't have time to get sick, and because of his high blood pressure and family history he couldn't afford too much stress.

When Jacob and I began our work together, he was a prime candidate for three-dimensional thinking and guilt-free play. "I can't possibly do it all," he said. And Jacob was somewhat surprised at first to hear me say, "That's right, you can't do it all. Nobody could do it *all at once.* You can only work on one job and one step at a time. That's all you ever can do. Which one makes sense to start on this after-noon? At what time do you choose to start this afternoon . . . on what small task . . . and for how long?"

After getting Jacob focused and in control of being overwhelmed, we needed to establish a firm commitment to stress-free, guilt-free oases of recuperation in his busy week. Jacob rapidly grasped the importance of the Now Habit tools and how to apply them. The Unschedule helped him prevent burnout and resistance by ensuring he'd have time for family and freedom from worry about the job; the work of worrying prepared him for potential problems and freed him from chronically considering the "what if's"; and the self-talk of choice and creating safety directed his thoughts toward what *he* chose to do and released him from the anxiety caused by threats and self-criticism.

Jacob learned to counter anxiety about important de-cisions and the tendency to run from work problems by asking himself questions that directed his attention to-ward what he could do: "When can I start? Where do I choose to work? On what part of the job will I be start-ing?"

These techniques helped with the mental processes, but Jacob needed to *feel* calm in the midst of innumerable pressures and risks. He needed to work in the flow state to reach a state of mind and a physical calm that would make it easier to apply his new tools. When Jacob learned the focusing exercise, the entire program really clicked for him. It became more than a mental concept and a linear discipline.

"I see and feel myself using my focusing exercise and beginning to work in the flow state. Within two minutes I will be at a special level, working stress-free; tapping into a broader perspective; using more of my brain; recalling my safety, my ability, and my focus on taking one more step."

The focusing exercise gave Jacob periodic two-minute breathers so he could stand back and evaluate the challenges he faced, allow himself time to push aside fears, remind himself that he didn't have to do it all at once, and consider alternatives. Focusing directed Jacob's thoughts to productive action steps he could take and created sanctuaries of quality work throughout his day. By linking these two-minute calming sessions with periods of quality work, Jacob was able to control his anxiety, deal quickly with unpleasant tasks, and achieve hours of working in the flow state. His perception of time changed, his energy was calm and focused, his solutions were more creative, and his concentration improved.

Working in the flow state will complement your other new tools, eliminating most, if not all, of the negative habits that previously kept you procrastinating, replacing them with positive work attitudes and habits that turn work into an opportunity for exciting, focused, and creative achievement.

8

Fine-Tuning
Your Progress

*Great works are performed, not by strength, but
perseverance.*

—SAMUEL JOHNSON

This chapter presents a series of powerful techniques for
overcoming the setbacks and obstacles to your progress
from procrastinator to producer. Any program of habit
change, if it is to continue working for you over time,
needs to be fine-tuned and tailored to fit you. It must
prepare you to cope with setbacks and give you the tools
to quickly turn them into *opportunities* that further, instead of delay, your progress. Each of us faces difficult
times during which we are more apt to turn to procrastination as a familiar crutch. During such times we must
remember not to criticize ourselves and to persist in using
our new tools for rechanneling negative impulses in a
direction that reinforces our new, healthy habits.

PLANNED SETBACKS

Completing the transformation from an old habit pattern
to a new, more productive behavior requires trying out
your wings in situations that were formerly difficult or

tempting. For example, you may be responsible for a large project that has been overwhelming you. Suddenly you find yourself using a number of old escape patterns, such as doing more research, taking more time for phone calls, or discovering ten other things that require immediate attention. Realizing that you are reverting to your former habits will be helpful, but to successfully rechannel this energy into building a new, more productive habit, you'll need a strategy and techniques you can use quickly.

It's not necessary to totally eliminate your old patterns or relinquish your old identity to learn a new behavior. In fact, you can use familiar patterns to alert you to the opportunity to exercise the choices you now have. You now know alternative ways of behaving. To strengthen your ability to switch more readily and confidently from the old pattern to the new, you may even want to *plan a controlled setback.*

Use planned setbacks to rehearse your reactions. Watch yourself closely and make a mental record of the thoughts and anxieties that send you escaping to procrastination. Go right ahead and use your preferred method of procrastinating, with full awareness that now you have the tools to control fear of work and to enhance your sense of achievement at starting. For instance, when faced with a large project, you can choose to procrastinate by doing more background work. Or you can consciously delay making a decision about a major purchase by allowing yourself to be overwhelmed by the innumerable steps required in making a perfect, mistake-proof choice.

To test yourself using a planned setback:

- Choose a project on which you are likely to procrastinate (paying bills, returning letters, home repairs, starting on your income tax return).

- Notice the warning signs of procrastination associated with this project (for example, being overwhelmed by all the steps involved in paying bills or income tax; feeling that life has become a long list of "have to's"; feeling deprived and isolated from fun and friends because you have to work).

- Consciously choose to procrastinate for a few hours to observe the self-statements that lead to guilt and self-criticism: "I don't know what's wrong with me. Why can't I finish anything? Am I going to procrastinate my life away? If I can't even pay the bills or answer letters I really must be a mess."

- Notice how this process of self-criticism leads to guilt, depression, and resentment while keeping you from paying just one bill, putting one stamp on an envelope, finding one file for your income tax.

Your planned setback will point out when you are most likely to procrastinate. You now know where your former habits lead. Your knowledge of the guilt, frustration, and dissatisfaction that result from your former pattern can motivate you to use your new skills at guilt-free play, the Unschedule, and working in the flow state.

Use your planned setback as an instant replay, observing your thoughts as if from a distance as you "wire in" the corrective Now Habit technique every time you spot a symptom of counterproductive thinking and action.

- Notice how the challenging self-statements of a producer ("I don't have to do this. I will *choose* to *start* now, or I will accept the consequences of choosing to delay") lead to feelings of power —choice and assertiveness against pressure— and to focusing on what you can do in manageable chunks.

- Use the Unschedule to put these strategies into operation by creating a realistic picture of the time available this week, assured guilt-free play, rewards for do-able periods of quality work, and a system for building on what you are achieving.

- Use the focusing exercise to help you rapidly and efficiently make the transition from overwhelmed to focused by reaching your deeper, creative self; taking time to remind yourself of positive suggestions and visualizations; and focusing in the present with choice, motivation, and interest.

RESILIENCE AND HARDINESS

I want to make sure that once you've gotten started on the road to becoming a producer you are not discouraged by a sudden problem. "Planned setbacks" allow you to build resilience (the ability to bounce back) and hardiness (the ability to withstand and avoid pitfalls) into the start, the middle, and the completion of your projects.

Resilience

People who consider themselves failures have failed once and stay there. A "failure" wants a guarantee before starting a project that everything will go perfectly, without any problems. A successful person is willing to take reasonable risks, knowing that there are no guarantees except Murphy's Law that "if something can go wrong, it will." Successful people fail many times and bounce back, refusing to let any one failure define their worth. In spite of the difficulties and failures they face in life, successful people learn to be resilient and carry on. They've developed a series of nets under their high-wire act that lets them know that *"A mistake will not be the end of the world because I won't let it be. I will pick myself up and will try again—regardless of how embarrassed or hurt I feel."*

Anytime you try something new and commit yourself to a course of action you can expect some setbacks. The possibility of setbacks is not an excuse to procrastinate. Setbacks are not another reason to worry about failure, and they certainly are not indicators of your worth as a person. Every path, every role, and every job in life has some difficulties. There are no perfect paths. Just because you find more work and problems on your path than you anticipated doesn't mean that you made a wrong choice or a mistake!

Remember to avoid self-criticism about setbacks or obstacles that appear in the midst of your project. As management consultant Michael Durst says, "You may not be responsible for causing what happens to you, but you are responsible for what you do to correct it." This powerful message contains a crucial concept that many people miss: let go of worrying about the initial cause of the problem so that you can direct your energies to where they can do the most good—the solution.

The ability to rapidly correct an error involves taking responsibility for the solution, but first you must let go of what I call the "why-whine"—"Why did this happen to me? Why am I always the one who gets the tough jobs?

Why can't I learn to do things right? Why am I destined to suffer the assaults of so many jerks?" This is another form of the "should's" and "shouldn't's" that delay your acknowledging the reality of your situation (regardless of how unpleasant), correcting it, lessening the difficulty, and avoiding it in the future.

In *Peak Performance*, Charles Garfield tells us that the trajectory of the Apollo moon rocket was off course 90 percent of the time. By acknowledging the deviations from the expected path, the scientists were able to repeatedly make the necessary corrections and achieve an imperfect, but adequate, trajectory to the moon. They achieved a major breakthrough by sticking to the mission in spite of numerous setbacks.

What distinguishes a champion from others of comparable ability is the learned skill of bouncing back from disappointing performances. Being a champion—a consistent producer—requires that you forgive yourself for errors and losing streaks while maintaining the sense of inner worth and safety necessary to solve problems and pursue your goals.

Sticking with the mission while adjusting to negative feedback is an essential skill in the repertoire of the long-term performer. Lee Iacocca's firing by Henry Ford II, for example, was a devastating setback that could have lead a lesser man to accept retirement. Iacocca, however, refused to stay devastated. Instead, he turned away from self-blame and chose to tackle the enormous financial and management problems then facing Chrysler. He chose taking risks and solving problems over worrying about possible failure and criticism. Iacocca wasn't born with this robustness; he learned it by trial and error, repeatedly bouncing back from errors to try again.

After much work on overcoming her previous procrastination patterns, Sarah, a chemist for a genetic engineering firm, developed a relaxed and creative style of working and was doing well on her new job. She was happy with most aspects of the job, but she had not been prepared for the politics, sexism, and favoritism practiced by the managers. She began to feel that her ability was not being appreciated and that her job required jumping certain hurdles to prove herself.

The progress she was making in adapting to her new job and in controlling procrastination was disrupted when her boss unexpectedly and harshly criticized her work. He said the wrong thing at the wrong time, and this revived Sarah's old fears and resentments: "Am I good enough? Can I do this job successfully? Nothing will please him, so why try?" The setting was ripe for the familiar cycle of resentment, resistance, fear, and perfectionism that leads to procrastination.

Anticipating further criticism and unfairness, Sarah began to withhold her skill and creativity from her projects and slowed down her work while preparing for further criticism and unfairness. She was back to her old crutch, procrastination, but now was able to recognize the underlying causes and quickly turned it around. This time she felt more in control of her reactions. She knew she had several techniques that had worked for her in less serious situations.

She realized that she had been criticizing herself for not anticipating the new job's shortcomings and for thinking that this was *the* perfect job. She needed to forgive herself for not knowing the job's drawbacks in advance. Rather than despairing that she had chosen the wrong job, Sarah could now see the job's difficulties as feedback that her expectations would need adjustment so she could better cope with the reality of the situation.

After weighing the pluses and minuses, Sarah decided to give the job six months, during which time she would make her best effort. She recommitted to the job and took full responsibility for her projects. Sarah also decided that she wasn't going to procrastinate about personal confrontations. She told her boss, "I took this job in good faith, feeling that I could make a contribution to this company. In the short time I've been here I have not been given the opportunity to demonstrate what I can do. I would like your cooperation in granting me the time and the authority to do my job and be judged on my efforts. If I find that within six months we are not in agreement about what I can do, I will leave of my own accord."

The boss was impressed, but perhaps more importantly, Sarah had gotten past her building resentment and procrastination. Rather than reverting to an old pattern just because of a setback, she applied her new strategies and techniques. She took control of the situation and refused to be put in the victim role. Sarah directly addressed the issue of her boss's unfairness and her own procrastination, using this setback as an opportunity to be resilient and bounce back, even when the obstacles had been placed by others.

Hardiness

Suzanne Kobasa, a professor at City University of New York, has identified what she calls "hardiness," a constellation of three personality characteristics—commitment, control, and challenge. Repeatedly, executives possessing these three characteristics have been shown to withstand stress and resist illness better than their peers who lack them.

Hardy individuals, rather than feeling alienated from their work, powerless over events, or threatened by change, tend to "easily commit themselves to what they are doing," "believe that they can at least partially control events," and "regard change to be a normal challenge or impetus to development . . ." Hardy executives have an overall life plan, flexible goals, and the ability to *turn stressful events into opportunities* that mitigate for them the disruption caused by any single stressful event.

To build hardiness into the way you cope with work projects, you can practice attitudes of commitment, control, and challenge in leisure activities such as exercise. As with Laura, whose experience in completing a marathon helped her discover a way to complete her research, you can use sports as a safe arena to try out building the habits of hardiness.

You might practice walking (or running, or any activity you're comfortable with) your designated distance, say two miles or forty-five minutes. Having completed your goal, walk an additional quarter-mile uphill. Walk it slowly, without self-talk about the difficulty in finishing. Notice how much easier it is after you've completed your goal. It won't seem as steep this time. Why? Because you've already achieved your goal. You *don't have to* walk the quarter-mile uphill; you're choosing to do it, and you're watching your energy level instead of your internal chatter about whether or not you can do it.

Notice that you're not trying to trick yourself about the reality of the hill; you're just taking control over your attitude and how you talk to yourself, and that changes your experience of reality. Be aware of how difficult that last quarter-mile can be when you're thinking about finishing, knowing that it's literally an uphill battle. Make note of any negative thoughts such as "I can't do it" or "This hurts too much." Practice getting past these thoughts and notice how you accomplish this.

This exercise will teach you that focusing solely on the

goal is tiring; maintaining inflexible goals makes it harder to proceed; and your energy level is affected by how you talk to yourself. You can go farther than you think you can.

Whenever your thoughts about work or projects seem overwhelming or defeating ("I can't do it; I don't know how I can accomplish this task"), remember how you dealt with that same feeling when you faced the hill. You really didn't know if you could do it, yet you persevered, focused on the small steps you *could* take, noticed a change in perspective and feeling, and completed the task of walking up the hill. Whether it's a hill or the annual budget, how you persevere in one area will build confidence in your use of hardiness in the rest of your life.

In discussing goal achievement and focusing techniques with marathon runners, I discovered that an essential part of their training as long-distance runners involves letting go of the goal and staying in the process—*for over two hours.* Many times during the 26-mile course, runners think, "I can't do it." But they're used to this kind of distraction and have prepared themselves to use such thoughts to remind themselves to focus on what they *can* do now. They are ready with a positive self-statement, such as "I'm going to finish even if I have to slow down and shuffle through the next few steps. Then I'll see if I can win."

One runner, an Olympic contender, told me, "If I think too much about reaching the finish line I lose speed, whether I'm ahead or behind. I've had to train myself to turn my attention away from finishing and toward the next step, the process of staying in the race."

In a very different arena, Nathaniel, an entrepreneur, reports,

> If I worry too much about maintaining my income and paying the bills I begin to delay on important decisions,

act too carefully, try to follow a safe formula. This interferes with my ability to think creatively and to act spontaneously. I found that taking a few minutes to focus helps me to become aware of the fears that normally would take control of how I feel. Once I'm aware of what's going on—that I'm worrying too much about making a mistake or getting too eager for a specific goal —I can realistically assess the risk and *choose* to take it or walk away from it. But at least now I'm in control, not my fears; I have a choice.

CONCENTRATION: CONTROLLING DISTRACTIONS

Overcoming procrastination while in the midst of a setback can be complicated by an inability to concentrate. Understanding and controlling distracting thoughts is important for fine-tuning your work habits and preparing you to cope effectively with setbacks.

Distracting thoughts may be creative and useful, they may be a release of suppressed emotion, or they may simply be random. Your mind is continually processing data and sensations for your protection, growth, and enlightenment. Yet there are times when the thoughts and images coursing through our mind seem more disruptive than useful. If you can anticipate them and develop a system for warding them off, you'll be better able to put distractions to use for you.

"My problem is that I can't concentrate. I get distracted whenever I try to work," a typical client will tell me. I often reply, "When *you* can't concentrate, what are your distracted thoughts concentrating on?" The point is that you cannot *not* concentrate. Thus, the problem is not that you *can't* concentrate, but that your attention is drawn to something you'd rather not be concentrating on or worrying about, such as your boss's potential criticism or how badly you'd like to be finished.

Certain types of distractions, such as strong emotions, need to be dealt with immediately, but the large majority of distractions can be dealt with *after* you complete some quality work. If you are having extreme difficulty concentrating, quickly jot down any distractions on a separate pad. Once you've completed some work, the craving will have subsided, regardless of how strong it was thirty minutes earlier. As you review your list of distracting thoughts and cravings, you will find, for the most part, that the urge to eat a bag of potato chips or to call a friend disappeared as soon as you got involved in your work. With the satisfaction of having started, you can—without guilt and under your own control—reward yourself by tackling those prior distractions you've written on your list.

In addition to rapidly refocusing your concentration on the task, listing your distracting thoughts will help you identify those that can be dismissed as simply creative ways to avoid something you're ambivalent about doing. For more serious distractions, it is important that you schedule a specific time to deal with them. During these scheduled times you can give proper attention to the questions that have been begging for resolution. As you begin keeping to your commitments to resolve such issues at a specified time, the frequency of the distracting reminders will lessen as your mind learns that you are taking care of business.

Dr. Martha Maxwell, in *Improving Student Learning Skills*, tells us that there are at least five types of distractions:

1. Strong Emotions. This is the one type of distraction that deserves your immediate attention. You may be using work as an attempt to distract yourself from facing strong emotions regarding a loved one, confrontations with difficult people, or medical or financial concerns. Rather than struggling to concentrate on work and continuing to procrastinate on dealing with these feelings, allow yourself some time (it can be as brief as ten minutes) to think through what you can do to cope with the situation or to change it. Also think about where you can get support and when you can contact friends. When you have acknowledged your emotions and developed some plan for coping with them, you will be better able to concentrate on work.

2. Warnings of Danger. Real or imagined threats will interrupt your ability to concentrate by stimulating an adrenaline reaction. To avoid the agitation caused by this type of distraction, challenge any pressure messages you've given yourself ("I have to finish by Wednesday, or else!") and remember that you have alternative ways of surviving even the worst that could happen. Removing threats and doing the work of worrying about any imagined catastrophes will reduce the stress response and its distracting warning signal.

3. "To-Do" Reminders. While you're immersed in a difficult project, that quart of milk you have to buy or some other "to-do" item will suddenly haunt you for no apparent reason. Procrastination on this form of distraction is quite legitimate. You can write down the distractions on your pad, relieving yourself of the burden of trying to remember, and deal with them later, after at least one-half hour of quality work. This process can make you extraordinarily efficient. You're using your "to-do" chores as rewards for completing work instead of as reasons to procrastinate.

4. Escape Fantasies. If you anticipate long periods of deprivation, you can expect an increase in fantasies about food, sex, and vacations. Record your escape fantasies to plan your future guilt-free play. Deciding to work on short, tolerable periods of work and making sure you have rewards and social events to look forward to on your Unschedule will minimize this type of distraction.

5. UFOs—Unidentified Flights of Originality. Creative, and often seductive thoughts that cannot be fathomed at this time may fly through your mind while you are working on a project. These may be very creative associations but they are probably not useful to you at this time. Let these UFOs fly by undisturbed, or quickly write them down so you can consider them later if you wish.

By identifying and recording distractions, you'll be keeping interruptions to a minimum. And because you know that the distractions will be dealt with soon if they're important, you'll be able to stay relaxed enough to concentrate on doing quality work on your current project.

MENTAL REHEARSAL AND PREPROGRAMMING

Mental imagery is a powerful tool in preparing you for possible danger. In learning to do the work of worrying, you used it to cope with anxiety by creating a plan for safety and survival. It is also extremely useful as a way of rehearsing your optimal performance on everyday tasks. Mental rehearsal and preprogramming are forms of mental imagery that can prepare you to push aside distractions and procrastination traps while targeting your attention on your goals.

One very successful businesswoman consulted me about a block she was experiencing with a particularly messy project that she estimated would take two to four weeks to straighten out. Martha was a delight to work with. She had quickly grasped the concepts of the Unschedule and guilt-free play and applied them to her company with her own unique flair and ingenuity. But she was having a devil of a time with one project about which she had an enormous sense of dread and resistance.

As Martha described the project with all of its twists and turns and potential for criticism from her boss, I began to understand her difficulty with starting to unravel this ball of knotted yarn. She had been very successful in using my concepts and techniques, so I had considerable credibility with her. Knowing this I said, "At the risk of sounding too 'New Age' and confused in psychobabble, I'd like you to close your eyes, take three slow breaths, and let go of trying to solve this dilemma at the conscious level. Just let your subconscious mind give you a picture and a feeling of this block. Notice how large it is, its shape, its thickness, its color."

Martha and her subconscious mind were very cooperative. She saw in her imagination a brick wall, thirty feet high and five feet thick, completely across her path. I asked Martha to slowly approach her block. (This is what you do with blocks, and bogey men, and monsters for that matter—you approach them.)

As she approached her wall and felt the solidness of its bricks, I asked Martha to expect a creative solution from her subconscious. It wasn't very long before she began to see a light shining through at one end of her wall, and there she found a small door that led to her project. The wall really was quite dense, but she now knew she could start on the project without having to first knock down that wall. Martha could keep her wall, yet she could get through it when she wanted to by entering that small door.

What a creative solution her mind had given her! Martha was delighted with herself and better understood how she needed both the protection that the wall provided and some flexibility. Previously she had seen it as an either-or situation: a powerful defensive block or a slavish compliance to the demands of her project. Now she had both.

The excitement of her release from fear and resentment made Martha eager to start early the next morning. When she decided on 8:00 A.M. as her starting time I asked her how realistic this was. After reconsidering, she committed to being at her desk, working on her project by 9:00 A.M. We then did a bit more mental rehearsal to ensure we had eliminated other potential obstacles to a successful start. With her eyes closed, Martha preprogrammed how she would organize her work: she visualized where she would find various files and notes; she used the feeling of her chair to remind her to use the focusing exercise to get through the early frustrations of starting; she really committed to her breaks, a good lunch, and an enjoyable evening; and she used her breathing throughout the day to refocus her energy and commitment whenever there was a snag.

When I saw Martha the following week, she was amazed at how well the mental rehearsal, focusing, and preprogramming had worked. She actually started at 8:45 and found the files right where she imagined them to be. She was off to a good start, with quality work on a complex task, by going around the block and the procrastination.

By using mental rehearsal you can find yourself remembering to start on your project at the preprogrammed time. You will have given your mind a picture it can grasp and a message it can cooperate with. It will draw you to the place you imagined for your chosen work. As you sit in that chair and see the actual clock, indicating the time you imagined in your rehearsal, you automatically begin to recall the pleasant feelings of your focusing exercise. Within two minutes you will be relaxed and focused, capable of retrieving the solutions that have been "seeded" by you and your creative faculty while you played and dreamed—you're using more of your brain to help you work more easily and rapidly. Your earlier mental rehearsal has prepared the neural pathways of your brain to facilitate optimal performance.

EFFECTIVE GOAL SETTING

*Nothing is so fatiguing as the eternal hanging on
of an uncompleted task.*

—WILLIAM JAMES

As you leave your old procrastination habits behind, you can turn your attention more readily toward achieving your goals. With the assistance of your new tools, you'll be able to undertake larger goals with greater confidence and with a greater chance of completing them. Rather than struggling with procrastination, you'll be more oriented toward results, and you'll want to select and set goals in a way that optimizes your chances of success.

How you set your goals strongly influences your ability to recommit to them and bounce back after a setback. A final set of steps is appropriate, therefore, to ensure effective goal setting that lessens problems with procrastination and enhances the ease with which you work and persevere along the path to achievement.

We all have a number of things we would like to accomplish, things we tell ourselves we "should" accomplish—increasing our net profits, learning to play the piano, making a million dollars, taking a vacation, writing a book, finishing a degree, repairing the house, losing ten pounds, spending more time with friends, getting up earlier. Given our limited amount of time and energy, we must make decisions and set priorities in order to make progress on *one* goal and to avoid disappointment and feelings of failure about the rest.

To ensure that your way of setting goals helps you overcome procrastination, make commitments only to those goals and paths that you can wholeheartedly embrace. To avoid the frustration of the procrastination cycle, you must abandon unattainable goals and half-hearted wishes.

If you have a number of goals that remain unfulfilled and that continue to plague you with guilty "shoulds"—"I should get in shape"; "I've got to get organized"; "I should fix the back door"; "I have to get around to dealing with customer complaints"—chances are that, though you want the goal, you have been unwilling to made a commitment to the work required to accomplish it or, even though you really *want* to do it, you can't find the time in your busy schedule.

One of the best-kept secrets of successful producers is their ability to let go of goals that cannot be achieved or started in the near future. To set realistic goals you must be willing to fully commit to working on the *path* to that goal and be capable of investing the time and energy required to start now. If you cannot find the time or motivation to start working on that goal, let go of it, or it will keep haunting you, making you feel like a procrastinator —as if you'd failed to accomplish something important that you're committed to.

Should you find that your interest in this goal persists but that you cannot start on it now, change your expectations of when or how you will achieve the goal. Consider it for your retirement "to-do" list or as something you can creatively daydream and procrastinate on; or think of it as a *wish* rather than a goal—something that may happen in a different way than you originally expected. Set a time, weeks or months from now, to reconsider the priority of this goal and your readiness to commit to starting work on it at that time, but *let go of it for now* so that you can focus on a present goal that is attainable and will bring you some sense of achievement.

Remember, *you are the master of your goals;* don't let unrealistic goals be used as an occasion for self-criticism and for lapsing into identifying yourself as a procrastinator. As a producer you know which goals to wholeheartedly pursue and which ones to let go of.

Avoiding Setbacks

Part of our hesitation to set goals comes from the knowledge that any time we make this kind of commitment we risk confronting setbacks and demands that will require us to stretch beyond our usual comfort limits. Setting a goal will require you to steer your activities in one direction, within a prescribed time period, along a path of challenges that will remind you of your human limits and frailties.

The following steps will help you to maintain the motivation necessary to complete your goal and the hardiness to handle the normal setbacks that are present on any journey toward a goal. These steps will apply Now Habit techniques to the task of setting goals effectively.

Recognize the work of procrastinating. Let go of the fantasy that you can escape work by procrastinating. There is no path in life that requires no effort. Prepare yourself for making a commitment to your goal by recognizing that there are costs involved in both working and trying to avoid work. The choice is not *working* or *not working,* but *which type of work;* even feeling guilty because of procrastinating takes some effort. When you commit to a goal, you're committing to a form of work that will bring rewards. When you procrastinate, you're choosing a self-punishing form of work.

Clearly, work is required when you decide on a goal, commit to the path, and continually stretch beyond your current abilities toward the goal. But it also takes work to feel unfulfilled and to maintain a list of unachieved resolutions.

Freely choose the entire goal. State your goal in the form of a choice or decision: "I freely choose to work on . . ." or "I will work on . . ." If a goal is important to you, and you know you are going to accomplish it one way or another, it makes sense to *freely choose all the work involved* in reaching that goal—the tedious work as well as the fun parts.

In fact, you may want to get through the boring or onerous parts (adding up of receipts for your income tax, the first mile of your workout, priming the woodwork) more quickly in order to experience a sense of control, to minimize the pain, and to reach the pleasurable parts. In *The Road Less Traveled,* M. Scott Peck writes of a procrastinating financial analyst who always started with the more pleasurable parts of tasks—including eating the icing on her cake first. He told her that if she tried to "accomplish the unpleasant part of her job during the first hour [of her workday], she would then be free to enjoy the other six." Dr. Peck explains, "It seemed to me, . . . that one hour of pain followed by six of pleasure was preferable to one hour of pleasure followed by six of pain. . . . Delaying gratification is a process of scheduling the pain and pleasure of life in such a way as to enhance the pleasure by meeting and experiencing the pain first and getting it over with."

Choosing to face the pain—because getting it out of the way allows you to start on the more pleasurable parts —makes all the difference in how you experience the task and how much you control any tendency to procrastinate. Making a free choice and firm decision to get through the task empowers and focuses you, changing your experience of the work. As Bill, a football player, said about his daily exercise routine, "I hate sit-ups. If I leave them for last I dread my entire workout. It ruins my attitude about the whole workout. However, when I decided to do my sit-ups first, they went faster and I actually enjoyed the rest of my workout. That small shift made a big difference in how I feel."

Create functional, observable goals. Vague goals must be translated into something tangible you can do. A realistic goal includes an action verb, a deadline, and a cost component, usually time or money. For example, "I will complete painting the house by June 1, by investing at least fifteen hours a week," or "I will lose ten pounds by December 31 by exercising thirty minutes a day and eating an average of 300 calories less a day." Divide your goal into action-oriented, clearly observable subgoals. For example, "I will make fifteen calls by 1:00 P.M. Wednesday" is preferable to "Get finished by sometime next week."

To be truly effective in your goal setting, you'll need a functional subgoal that tells you what to do *today* in order to get closer to that ultimate goal. Action-oriented subgoals will help you to visualize when, where, and on what you need to start each day to achieve your goal by a certain deadline.

If you simply stay with your ultimate goal, as is typical of ineffective goal setting, you'll have only a vague sense of what you need to do, and there's a great danger that you will be overwhelmed by the amount of work involved.

A LAST WORD

Experiment with the techniques presented throughout this book. Fine-tune them to fit your personal style and your situation. Stay open to change, with the assurance that you have the new tools of the Now Habit to replace old procrastination patterns and underachievement. Avoid statements such as "I'll *try* it" or "It's not working," which reveal a testing attitude rather than a firm commitment. The feeling behind "I'll try" is that you will make a halfhearted effort and then fail. Defeatist statements such as "It's not working" mean you've failed to find a tool to take away *all* the anxiety, that once again your problem remains unsolved, and that you are likely to rely on your old attempted solution, procrastination, to escape fear and discomfort. "How can I make this work for me?" reflects a greater commitment and drive toward success.

I hope you'll use the Now Habit program to get in touch with your own abilities, motivation, and inner genius. With the Now Habit as your ally, look forward to having a positive attitude toward work, control over procrastination, resiliency against setbacks, and a new identity as a producer.

9

The Procrastinator in Your Life

All of us must work with, live with, and relate to individuals whose own problems with procrastination affect us negatively: the mate who is consistently late for dinner; the employee who must be reminded several times that reports are due; the friend who fails to return telephone calls. Unless we have a firm grasp of the basic causes and patterns of procrastination (chapters 1 and 2), most of us will unwittingly reinforce procrastination patterns in those whom we manage, counsel, and love.

We try to instruct our spouses, friends, and employees about the importance of being on time and meeting deadlines, but to no avail. Somehow we can't get through to them, and, as if to spite us, they seem to get worse. "When will you get organized?" we shout in desperation to those who heed neither our wise counsel nor our threats. In *Procrastination: Why You Do It, What to Do About It,* psychologists Jane Burka and Lenora Yuen state, "In all your interactions with procrastinators, try to function as *consultant,* and not as a director. In other words, offer your support, be a sounding board, and help procrastinators be realistic but don't try to decide things for them or judge their moral character."

MANAGING PEOPLE
WHO PROCRASTINATE

Procrastination causes our industries millions in lost hours of work and forces them to let go of many thousands of potentially valuable employees. The daily efficiency and quality of our productivity is affected by this habit and by ineffectual attempts at managing it. To be effective in managing people who procrastinate, you must direct them toward choice, safety, and acknowledgment for what they can do, and you must avoid making those critical statements with which procrastinators are all too familiar. The critical inner dialogue that is learned in childhood can persist into adulthood, as demonstrated in Garrison Keillor's story in *Lake Wobegon Days* of a young man whose parents communicated with him mostly through criticism and the withholding of praise.

> You never paid a compliment, and when other people did, you beat it away from me with a stick . . . "That's wonderful that he got that job." [To which his parents would reply,] "Yeah, well, we'll see how long it lasts." You trained me so well, I now perform this service for myself. I deflect every kind word directed to me, and my denials are much more extravagant than the praise.

Remember that the procrastinator's poor self-image and ineffective attempts at motivation result in a continual internal dialogue such as "I *have to finish* something *important* and do it *perfectly* while enduring long periods of *isolation* from the people and things I love." This makes procrastinators much better dictators toward themselves than any outsider could ever hope to be. The results-oriented manager, therefore, resists using such messages as "You have to finish this important job, and there'd better be no mistakes," which would only contribute to procrastinators' self-imposed pressure, criticism, and threats and to greater blocks to action.

Employers and managers, in particular, can be more effective in controlling procrastination by being mindful of the counterproductive self-talk procrastinators use with themselves (see chapter 3) so that they are prepared to counter their unproductive focus with statements that channel their energy toward results.

The ability to communicate in the language, images, and emotions that evoke understanding, inspiration, and direction in the governed is the hallmark of effective leadership. The effective manager, coach, or leader can empathize with the various learning styles and emotional perspectives of the governed.

Winning coaches, for example, recognize the different learning styles of their players. Former Raiders coach John Madden says that for some players you simply tell them the play and they immediately know it; others must be shown diagrams before they can form their own mental image of what to do; and still others won't really grasp the play until they physically run through it so that they can *feel* the play, as well as *see* and *hear* it. The same is true for the "coaches" of military recruits and corporate training programs. The effective coaches understand employees' motivations, fears, and attempted solutions. They ensure that their communications address these needs and fears and reduce employee reliance on counterproductive solutions such as procrastination.

To work effectively with procrastinators—and that means most people—managers must keep in mind the three main issues that are at the bottom of most procrastination problems: feeling like a victim; being overwhelmed; and fear of failure. Successful leaders and managers address these problem areas by communicating in terms that elicit commitment rather than compliance, by focusing on manageable objectives rather than on overwhelming expectations, and by providing praise for steps taken in the right direction rather than just criticising mistakes. Their management style creates a pull toward the goal, focuses on starting each step, and provides adequate safety and rewards.

COMMITMENT VS. COMPLIANCE

Commitment to a task sparks much more creativity and motivation than *compliance.* Management through compliance places a heavy burden on the manager to maintain sufficient authority and force to have workers acquiesce to orders without question. Douglas McGregor, in *The Professional Manager,* states that coercive management styles, while working to some extent, tend to produce unintended negative side effects in employees. Among these are antagonism to and noncompliance with rules, apathy, an increased need for close supervision, and higher administrative costs.

Demands for Compliance

"You'd better be finished by noon."

"You have to get here on time, or else."

"You should do it exactly as I showed you."

"I'm in charge, so just do as you're told."

Injunctions of "have to" and "should" imply a threat from an outside authority that is forcing a victim to do something against his or her will. These demand messages result in feelings of powerlessness, ambivalence, resentment, and resistance that frequently find expression through procrastination. Procrastination can be drastically reduced by offering employees legitimate outlets to express their power and control over work projects rather than the passive resistance of procrastination.

Allowing employees to participate in decisions that affect their work and giving them choices over how they carry out orders creates a sense of commitment. This leads to a greater sense of personal responsibility for quality work than a "take it or leave it" attitude that demands only compliance.

When employees can be more than victims, passively complying with demands and threats, they can drop resistance to authority and commit their motivation and creativity to getting the job done rather than avoiding punishment.

Inviting Commitment

"What can you get to me in rough form by noon?"

"I've placed you in a responsible position, and I'm depending on you to be here at nine o'clock."

"We need to be able to trust each other's work, so I need you to follow the guidelines precisely. Let me know if you have any problems with them."

"I have responsibility for this unit, but there are things I don't see—blind spots in my way of working—so I need your help in keeping me informed if I miss some things."

As a manager, you maintain control over *when* the task is completed and the quality of the work, but you can't do it all. To be truly effective and efficient you must delegate to trusted employees. In order to get the results when you need them, you must communicate to your workers that they are entrusted with the responsibility *and the authority* to participate, with full commitment to the task.

FOCUSING ON STARTING VS. FINISHING

The enormity of the work involved in meeting distant deadlines for large or important tasks will evoke anxiety in procrastinators as they either try to do it all at once or avoid even starting. In some people, the tendency to become anxious and overwhelmed is so great that any task extending beyond a week's work will require managers to carefully structure tasks into manageable parts that can be started immediately, and to avoid statements that place an inordinate amount of emphasis on finishing.

Emphasis on Finishing

"When will you finish this project?"

"You've got to complete this by Friday."

"There's a lot to get done."

"Remember, that deadline is only two months away."

While these statements have the advantage of being direct, they show a lack of understanding of the procrastinator's problems with being too overwhelmed to start, establishing realistic time limits, making judgments as to when the quality of the project is good enough, and knowing how to make the decisions required to finish on time. They also leave the procrastinator focused on the finishing point as the goal, somewhere in the distant future, without an agreed-upon starting point. With such vague commands, you could propel the perfectionist into creating a much more elaborate and expensive project than is necessary to meet your needs.

Effective managers understand the importance of communicating to their employees the specific action steps required to begin the task. They also understand that overcoming inertia is half the battle. With employees who have difficulty starting, effective managers take time to ascertain the possible causes of blocks—wasting time trying to be perfect, being overwhelmed by trying to tackle the entire task, failing to create a three-dimensional schedule of the subgoals, and a clear image of when and where to start. With a three-dimensional picture of the subgoals and subdeadlines, both you and the procrastinators you supervise will know what work is due when.

Being Clear About Where to Start

"When can you start on a very rough draft?"

"I need this by next Friday. Plan to have a rough sketch to me in time for our meeting on Tuesday at ten o'clock so we can go over it together."

"Would you draw up a rough agenda of the necessary steps for closing the Jones account, and have it for me by three o'clock? Then we can set a realistic time frame for its completion."

"If we're going to meet that deadline of two months on the Smith case, I'll need to see at least an outline by Friday. Do you need someone to take over your other responsibilities while you get started?"

The responses you receive to these questions will let you know if you have properly communicated your sense of urgency about the project and the level of quality that is needed for your first review. The questions will focus the employees' attention on a small project that can be started now and reviewed in the near future. Their responses to your questions will also help you to clarify your own priorities and timetable for the project.

In these examples the manager has circumvented the procrastinator's tendency to fret about doing a perfect draft and has established and modeled the use of a three-dimensional path—from rough draft to finished product—to avoid creating feelings of being overwhelmed. Thus the employee, instead of being faced with a frightening and paralyzing "final judgment" at the end of the project, can think in terms of several progress reports. Each meeting with the manager helps to share responsibility for this important project and to serve as an opportunity for further feedback and direction upon which to build succeeding steps.

Dr. Leonard R. Sayles, professor of management at Columbia University, says that while "most managers see themselves as decision makers and order givers . . . this is an unrealistically passive view of what managers really have to do, since there can be serious problems in getting an order across to a subordinate. No matter how carefully phrased, many important orders require complex implementations. . . . the boss must keep initiating and *listening*. While the order may be clear, it takes on real meaning only as the boss watches a number of subsidiary choices or trade-offs the subordinate makes . . . and keeps nudging him toward the interpretation the boss intended when the order was given." Dr. Sayles further suggests that misinterpretations by the subordinate often have more to do with a failure to maintain a clear channel of communication with the boss rather than poor motivation on the part of the subordinate.

GETTING RESULTS OR GIVING CRITICISM

When managers criticize employees or threaten their job security in order to vent anger or in vain attempts at motivation, they are likely to impose blocks to productivity and contribute to procrastination. Employees who must constantly wonder "Will this be good enough to avoid being called on the carpet again? Will I be fired if I fail?" cannot use their full capacity for productive work, because their attention is compromised by necessary worries about surviving the boss's rages and maintaining their own self-respect. Workers' fears about their employer's judgments of their character, worth, and deservedness must be minimized to achieve maximum efficiency.

Criticism of the Person

"You can't do it right, what's wrong with you?"

"This report is totally off the point. You'll never get it done this way."

"That's just like you, you're always late."

"You really screwed up this time."

Statements such as these provoke stress through personal attacks and broad, counterproductive criticism that fails to point the way to corrective action. Rather than being distracted by attacks on their character, workers must be allowed to focus on what is required to get the job started (and completed). Clearly, an employee's personal insecurity is not the manager's problem. Yet it is within the manager's realm of responsibility to create a work environment that focuses on the task and on rapidly correcting errors, rather than on judgment of the employee and placing the blame. When errors do occur, criticism and threats must be avoided in favor of reassurances that if the employee is willing to learn, training will be freely given; that some drop in productivity is an acceptable part of learning a new job; and that management's focus is on teaching how goals are to be achieved rather than just giving orders and placing blame.

People learn faster in an environment where praise for steps in the right direction is abundant and criticism is kept constructive and focused on an area that can be improved. Whenever possible, commendations should be in writing so that they have added significance for the recipient and motivate fellow employees. As in the following examples, praise should precede even the mildest form of recommendation for improvement.

Praise

"I really liked what you did with the Jones account."

"The write-up was clear and concise."

"You maintained good follow-through on the phone with Mr. Jones."

"You did a good job handling the customer service problems."

Needs Improvement

> "I really liked what you did with the Jones account. And I think you can achieve even better results—and avoid some tension on your next project—if you follow the usual deadlines for informing the central office."

> "Your write-up was terrific. It was clear, concise, and on target. With some minor work on the last session, it will be excellent."

> "You maintained good follow-through on the phone with Mr. Jones. And I'd like you to really cement that contact by a personal visit to his plant. Next time when you're assigned a new account, set up a site visit as soon as possible."

> "You did a good job handling the customer service problems, and I'd like to see if more can be done to prevent those complaints."

The point of combining constructive recommendations for improvement with praise is that it tells workers more clearly which actions are correct and which ones need further effort, without causing undo stress that disrupts their ability to learn. When recognition for a job well done precedes any criticism, it lessens fear of failure about mistakes; recognizes that subordinates are doing something right and that their efforts are appreciated; and gives direction that is less likely to offend and is more likely to be heard as useful instruction on how to accomplish organizational objectives.

T. O. Jacobs in his seminal work on leadership, *Leadership and Exchange in Formal Organizations,* states that the first requirement for a leader is the establishment of mutual trust through consistency in delivering rewards as they are earned. The violation of this trust by a leader's arbitrary or inconsistent behavior leads to strong feelings of resentment, anger, and revenge on the part of employees—factors that are among the underlying causes of procrastination. This principle of consistency involves more than just fairness. It requires that managers select the right goals; define expectations clearly; help employees achieve their goals through technical competence and planning to avoid or overcome obstacles; and know which rewards are reasonable for a given effort.

The following guidelines will help managers improve productivity and avoid commands and actions that contribute to procrastination. These guidelines are in keeping with the Now Habit program and T. O. Jacobs's qualities of leadership that stimulate high levels of motivation in workers.

State Your Priorities Clearly

Let your staff know which work has priority and stick to it. If you repeatedly violate your priorities by presenting your workers with frequent emergencies, you lose credibility and teach your staff to procrastinate while they anticipate the next emergency. Cut down on your use of emergencies and crises as standard operating procedure. Use greater discrimination in assigning the label "emergency." When it is necessary to rearrange priorities, distribute your legitimate emergencies among different employees with proper support and relief from other assignments: "Give the Jones case top priority and put everything else on the back burner. Use whatever help you need to reassign your other cases."

Be Decisive

Don't be like the general who repeatedly changes his mind about where the foxholes should be dug and thus encourages malingering among his troops. Asking your workers to repeat difficult and complex tasks wastes their efforts and reinforces procrastination. Build confidence in your leadership by considering your decisions carefully, standing behind them, and clearly making known tasks that will result in meeting the organizational objectives.

If you are unsure of which work should be done, encourage your subordinates to participate in the decision-making process by asking them for rough drafts of several plans, rather than prematurely insisting on a finished product: "We can go several ways with the XYZ offer. I'd like to see the results of your brainstorming by noon so I can determine the best approach."

Be Fair and Frequent in Your Rewards

William James, Harvard's and America's first professor of psychology, said that the craving to be appreciated is a deep need in human nature. Small acknowledgments from someone in a position of authority go a long way in satisfying this need and have a large impact on an employee's sense of purpose and belonging in the firm. Frequent encouragement helps a worker to feel motivated *now* while on the path to distant rewards. Use subgoals and subdeadlines to give a greater sense of achievement and as an opportunity to offer rewards or direction along the way to the completion of the big task. Use *scheduled* meetings as opportunities to reward progress and to give constructive feedback on any movement in the desired direction: "Adams, I'm really impressed with what you have accomplished so far. With a bit of polishing and the addition of some graphs, it will be an outstanding presentation. When would you like to schedule our next meeting to discuss these changes?"

Give Constructive Feedback

Keep feedback focused on achieving the goal. When mistakes occur, express your disappointment at your mutual failure to communicate clearly and to achieve your mutual goals. But keep it focused on what needs to be done to make the necessary corrections to achieve the goal and to avoid the same errors in the future: "This is unacceptable. We really got our wires crossed on this one. The next time a customer says 'rough-grade lumber,' make sure you know what they mean. You'll need an interpreter with some of them. See if we can use the excess on another job before trying to return it to the lumberyard."

LIVING WITH A PROCRASTINATOR

Erma Bombeck suggests that if you live with someone who suffers from what she calls the "Sorry-I'm-Late Syndrome," you must resign yourself to never seeing the bride walk down the aisle, never seeing the opening moments of a movie, and never hearing the national anthem at the ball game.

Couples have been known to fight over such issues for years, and some even split up because of missed parties and chronic procrastination. So we vacillate between pleading and making threats. Being put in the role of the one who feels responsible for nagging is almost as bad as being nagged. Nagging only creates resentment in both parties: a feeling of pressure from an outside authority that must be rebelled against, on the one hand, and a feeling of being manipulated into playing cop or parent on the other.

Being nagged often places procrastinators in the position of children, who feel diminished by being told what to do. Fighting an authority figure then becomes more important than getting to the party on time and enjoying themselves. When, however, they are spoken to as if they are responsible and self-determining adults ("I'm leaving at eight o'clock") the procrastinators in your life can then *choose* to accompany you or allow you to leave alone. This opportunity to choose prevents their feeling like a victim who must respond to *your* sense of time pressure.

Though the procrastination patterns of a loved one may directly affect you, it is important that you not take them as personal affronts. Dealing with perfectionism, fear of failure and success, and the other underlying causes of procrastination makes it extremely difficult for most procrastinators to maintain a realistic idea of how much time it will take for them to complete a task.

They often unconsciously test you to see how much time they *really* have—time to avoid fearsome tasks and to exercise perfectionistic rituals in an attempt to stave off anticipated criticism. This means that, for procrastinators, "The dinner is at eight o'clock" is not quite as helpful as "We need to have the kids rounded up by 7:00 and leave at 7:30." Your own use of three-dimensional thinking and the reverse calender (covered in chapter 5) will help you communicate to the procrastinator in your life an image of the steps necessary for arriving at your destination on time.

On the other hand, the procrastinators shouldn't take it personally if you leave exactly when you say you're going to leave rather than waiting for them. You might explain how, through no real fault of your own, you are rather neurotic about being on time. You hope they understand and forgive you your little obsession, but it is better for your relationship with them if you can leave when you say you're going to leave.

Remember, this whole issue of being on time is *your* problem. Blaming the procrastinator is both ineffective and inappropriate. You will be more effective if you confess your little quirk about being on time: "I am not as adaptable and spontaneous as you are and therefore feel compelled to start now preparing for upcoming deadlines." While you're at it, you might as well admit that you're so obsessed with control that you have to use a "reverse calendar" approach for arriving on time at a wedding or movie. You're so human and imperfect, in fact, that you need this crutch to realistically consider how much time you will need to prepare and how much time the traffic will require. Your compassion for your neurotic side is such that you start when you say you're starting in order to avoid getting too anxious. "I'm not as good as you are with all the excitement of last-minute preparations," you might add. Now that you've gotten their attention, you can honestly ask for their understanding and cooperation in helping you keep your anxiety under control.

A couple who were clearly a case of opposites attracting came to see me about their conflicts over procrastination. David was always neat as a pin, punctual, and organized. His training as an engineer and his upbringing in a sensible, if somewhat repressed, family of scientists led him to believe that everyone should work as directly and efficiently as he. The early family experience and background of his wife, Karen, couldn't have been more different. Karen's family owned a small grocery store that functioned around, and in spite of, the family's many emotional storms. Her choice of social work as a career seemed almost as predestined as David's choice of engineering.

The more often David told Karen how important it was for her to be on time, the more she felt like a child being pressured by an angry parent or teacher. The more critical David was, the more she felt miserable, guilty, and confused about what to do. Within six months of meeting David, Karen, who had once run her own life effectively and successfully, had become a fumbling child about everyday chores such as balancing the checkbook, remembering to fill the gas tank, and keeping track of appointments.

David unknowingly had fallen into the role of the authoritarian who echoes the "should's" and "have to's" of life. What he could not know was that he was feeding into Karen's fears of rejection for being less than perfect and her own internal parental voice, which was even more demanding and critical than David. Karen reacted by taking on the roles of victim and passive resister. Without an awareness of the pressure/procrastination cycle, David and Karen were stuck in a frustrating tug of war. One would throw out a demand, and the other would feel compelled to pick up the gauntlet and engage in battle.

In our sessions, the underlying causes of procrastination were explained (see chapter 1) to impress upon both of them that procrastination is not a character flaw but a learned protective reaction to pressure, feeling overwhelmed, and fear of failure and of success. I wanted David and Karen to grasp the fact that if these underlying fears could be allayed, the learned tactic of procrastination could rapidly be unlearned.

It was essential that David be more committed to results than to making Karen conform to his idea of how a person should work and deal with deadlines. He also needed to understand that his playing the parental, pressuring role was counterproductive and unattractive. Karen needed to maintain her sense of power and avoid the passive resistance of the victim role. She also needed to regain the confidence in her way of accomplishing objectives she had had before David's criticism and pressure worsened her relatively minor problems with procrastination.

The first assignment I gave them seemed easier than it was in practice. I asked both of them to refrain from nagging, giving advice, and reminders about what the other needed to get done. They failed several times, but just trying to avoid these behaviors made each of them aware of how much of their communication was parental in nature and how well the other got along without being advised or reminded. This exercise renewed their respect for each other's mature and responsible behavior and pointed out areas where their priorities differed. David, for example, held the care of the family car at a much higher priority than Karen did, while she attributed a higher value than David to being at a dinner party on time. These differences in values and perspectives needed to be respected so that they could clearly communicate in terms of "I want, I choose, I have decided"—that is, the direct expression of empowerment without threat or demand that the other should conform. Direct statements of "I would like you to put gas in the car" or "I would like to leave at 7:00 P.M. for the Smiths' " soon replaced "You should remember to put gas in the car. What's wrong with you?" or "We're going to be late again. Why can't you be on time for anything that's important to me?"

While both David and Karen continued to procrastinate on some of their own tasks, they developed a sensitivity to each other's priorities, listened more carefully to nonblaming requests, recognized the nagging trap, and helped each other overcome procrastination by giving clear pictures of where to start on a project. They also learned to assert their individual needs while respecting the other's values, becoming more interested in results than in blame or control. Even if the procrastinators in your life don't get around to reading this book, your use of Now Habit strategies will clarify your communication and model for them the quality work and guilt-free play of a producer.

Bibliography

Allport, Gordon. *Becoming: Basic Considerations for a Psychology of Personality*. New Haven: Yale University Press, 1955.

Bandura, Albert. "The Self System in Reciprocal Determinism." *American Psychologist*, 1978, *33*, 344–358.

Beery, Rich G. "Fear of Failure in the Student Experience." *Personnel and Guidance Journal*, 1975, *54*, 190–203.

Bolen, Jean Shinoda. *The Tao of Psychology: Synchronicity and the Self*. New York: Harper & Row, 1979.

Bliss, Edwin C. *Getting Things Done: The ABC's of Time Management*. New York: Bantam, 1978.

Burka, Jane and Yuen, Lenora. *Procrastination: Why You Do It, What to Do About It*. Menlo Park, Calif.: Addison Wesley, 1984.

Cousins, Norman. *Anatomy of an Illness as Perceived by the Patient*. New York: Bantam, 1981.

——— *The Healing Heart*. New York: W. W. Norton & Company, Inc., 1983.

Davis, Martha; McKay, Mathew; Eschelman, Elizabeth. *The Relaxation & Stress Reduction Handbook*. Richmond, Calif.: New Harbinger, 1980.

Ellis, A. and Knaus, W. J. *Overcoming Procrastination*. New York: Signet, 1977.

Fiore, Neil A. *The Road Back to Health: Coping with the Emotional Side of Cancer*. New York: Bantam, 1986.

———and Pescar, Susan C. *Conquering Test Anxiety*. New York: Warner Books, 1987.

Fox, Matthew. *Original Blessing*. Santa Fe, New Mexico: Bear & Co., 1983.

Fromm, Eric. *Man for Himself*. New York: Holt, Rinehart, & Winston, 1947.

Garfield, Charles A. with Bennett, Hal Zina. *Peak Performance: Mental Training Techniques of the World's Greatest Athletes*. Los Angeles: Jeremy P. Tarcher, Inc., 1984.

Girdano, Daniel A. & Everly, George S. *Controlling Stress and Tension*. Englewood Cliffs, New Jersey: Prentice Hall, 1986.

Goleman, Daniel. "Concentration Is Likened to Euphoric States of Mind." *The New York Times*, March 4, 1986, pp. 21–22.

Griffin, Susan. *Pornography and Silence: Culture's Revenge Against Nature*. New York: Harper & Row, 1981.

Jacobs, T. O. *Leadership and Exchange in Formal Organizations*. Alexandria, Virginia: Human Resources Research Organization, 1971.

James, William. "The Energies of Men." *Memories and Studies*, edited by H. James, Jr. New York: Longmans, Green & Company, 1911.

Jampolsky, Gerald. *Love Is Letting Go of Fear*. Millbrae, Calif.: Celestial Arts, 1979.

Jaynes, Julian. *The Origin of Consciousness in the Break-*

down of the Bicameral Mind. Boston: Houghton Mifflin, 1976.

Kanfer, Frederick H. and Phillips, Jeanne S. *Learning Foundations of Behavior Therapy.* New York: John Wiley & Sons, 1970.

Keillor, Garrison. *Lake Wobegon Days.* New York: Penguin, 1985.

Knaus, W. J. *Do It Now: How to Stop Procrastinating.* Englewood Cliffs, N.J.: Prentice-Hall, 1979.

Kobasa, Suzanne C. "The Hardy Personality: Toward a Social Psychology of Stress and Health." *Social Psychology of Health and Illness,* edited by Glenn S. Sanders and Jerry Suls. Hillsdale, N.J.: Lawrence Erlbaum Associates, 1982, pp. 3–32.

————. "Stressful Life Events, Personality and Health: An Inquiry into Hardiness." *Journal of Personality and Social Psychology,* 1979, *37,* 1–11.

————and Puccetti, Mark C. "Personality and Social Resources in Stress Resistance." *Journal of Personality and Social Psychology,* 1983, *45* (4), 839–850.

Lakein, Alan. *How to Get Control of Your Time and Your Life.* New York: Signet, 1973.

Linville, Patricia W. "Self-Complexity as a Cognitive Buffer Against Stress-Related Illness and Depression." *Journal of Personality and Social Psychology,* 1987, *52* (4), 663–676.

Machlowitz, Marilyn. *Workaholics: Living with Them, Working with Them.* New York: Addison-Wesley, 1980.

Maslow, Abraham H. *Motivation and Personality.* New York: Harper & Row: 1970.

Maxwell, Martha. *Improving Student Learning Skills.* San Francisco: Jossey-Bass, 1979.

McGregor, Douglas. *The Professional Manager.* New York: McGraw-Hill, 1967.

————. *The Human Side of Enterprise.* New York: McGraw-Hill, 1960.

McLean, Alan A., M.D. *Work Stress.* Menlo Park, Calif.: Addison-Wesley Publishing Company, 1979.

Miller, Alice. *For Your Own Good: Hidden Cruelty in Child-Rearing and the Roots of Violence.* New York: Farrar, Straus, Giroux, 1983.

Minninger, Joan. *Free Yourself to Remember.* San Francisco: Workshops for Innovative Teaching, Inc., 1984.

————. *Total Recall: How to Boost Your Memory Power.* Emmaus, Pa: Rodale Press, 1984.

Peck, M. Scott. *The Road Less Traveled.* New York: Touchstone, 1978.

Poppy, John. "The Keys to Mastery," *Esquire.* May 1987, 107 (5), 119–126.

Porat, S. *Creative Procrastination: Organizing Your Own Life.* San Francisco: Harper & Row, 1980.

Restak, Richard. *The Brain.* New York: Bantam, 1984.

Rubin, Theodore I., M.D. *Compassion and Self-Hate.* New York: Ballantine, 1976.

Sayles, Leonard R. "Better Communicating . . . to Subordinates . . . to the Boss." *Boardroom Reports.* August 1, 1987, p. 10.

Schechter, David. "Complex Characters Handle Stress Better." *Psychology Today.* October, 1987, p. 26.

Suinn, Richard M. *Seven Steps to Peak Performance.* Lewiston, N.Y.: Hogrefe International, 1986.

Waitley, Denis. *The Psychology of Winning.* New York: Berkley Publishing, 1984.

—— and Witt, Reni. *The Joy of Working: The Thirty Day System to Success, Wealth and Happiness on the Job.* New York: Ballantine, 1986.

Watzlawick, Paul, Weakland, John and Fisch, Richard. *Change: Principles of Problem Formation and Problem Resolution.* New York: Norton, 1974.

Winnicott, Donald W. *Playing and Reality.* London: Tavistock, England, 1982.

Winston, Stephanie. *Getting Organized.* New York: Warner, 1978.

Von Oech, Roger. *A Whack on the Side of the Head: How to Unlock Your Mind for Innovation.* New York: Warner Books, 1983.

Zdenek, Marilee. *The Right-Brain Experience: An Intimate Program to Free the Powers of Your Imagination.* New York: Bantam, 1983.

ABOUT THE AUTHOR

Neil A. Fiore, Ph.D., is a management consultant and licensed psychologist in private practice in Berkeley, California. He has served as a psychologist at the University of California and as a consultant to industry and health and educational institutions. He has been published in *The New England Journal of Medicine, Science Digest,* and *Boardroom Reports,* and has appeared on numerous radio and television programs across the country. Dr. Fiore is widely acknowledged as an expert in the areas of health psychology, optimal performance, stress management, and hypnosis.